BOXING
in New Jersey,
1900–1999

BOXING
in New Jersey,
1900–1999

ROBERT F. FERNANDEZ, SR.

With a Foreword by
Peter R. Nozza *and*
Thomas A. Kaczmarek

McFarland & Company, Inc., Publishers
Jefferson, North Carolina

LIBRARY OF CONGRESS CATALOGUING-IN-PUBLICATION DATA

Fernandez, Robert F., Sr.
    Boxing in New Jersey, 1900–1999 / Robert F. Fernandez ;
with a foreword by Peter R. Nozza and Thomas A. Kaczmarek.
        p.   cm.
    Includes index.

    ISBN 978-0-7864-9476-7 (softcover : acid free paper) ∞
    ISBN 978-1-4766-1607-0 (ebook)

    1. Boxing—New Jersey—History.   2. Boxers (Sports)—New
Jersey—Biography.   I. Title.
    GV1125.F47 2014
    796.8309749090'49—dc23   2014026749

BRITISH LIBRARY CATALOGUING DATA ARE AVAILABLE

Cover image © 2014 Goodshoot

Printed in the United States of America

*McFarland & Company, Inc., Publishers
    Box 611, Jefferson, North Carolina 28640
    www.mcfarlandpub.com*

It is with great pride and honor that I dedicate
this book to Peter Nozza and Tommy Kaczmarek,
two great gentlemen whose belief in me is beyond words.
Boxing runs in their blood as it does in mine.
It was they who insisted that I write my boxing stories
down so others could enjoy them. Their advice and
wisdom I have followed, with their unending support.

Table of Contents

Table of Contents

Foreword

PETER R. NOZZA and
THOMAS A. KACZMAREK

Boxing is unparalleled in the realm of major sports, with unrestrained, explosive action that inspires spontaneous eruptions of emotions in its fans. Much has been written about the sport. However, immeasurable knowledge and history of the subject are the earmarks of a classic, profound and penetrating author, with the innate ability to compel a reader's interest. Moreover, a defining word in assessing literary work is passion.

Our far-reaching relationship with the author, Bob Fernandez, prompts us to assure the reader that Bob's knowledge of boxing and history, authentic writing style and passion for the sport are unsurpassed. These attributes are reflected throughout this masterwork, with vivid descriptions and recall of obscure circumstances.

Bob became obsessed with boxing bouts, history and memorabilia at a very early age. He has awed boxing enthusiasts and professionals for many years, with his detailed anecdotes and instant observations of fighters and boxing events, a veritable fount of boxing expertise.

Bob's multifaceted boxing knowledge was acquired firsthand, attending innumerable boxing shows and talking with fighters, trainers and managers in gyms and training camps.

A few of the great fighters Bob saw fight were his idols, including Sugar Ray Robinson, Muhammad Ali, Ike Williams, Beau Jack and Tippy Larkin, as well as countless local favorites.

His affinity for the sweet science is underscored as a highly recognized collector of boxing memorabilia, a meticulous labor of love that started at the age of ten. While passing a tavern with his mother and see-

1

ing a Zale-vs.-Graziano poster, he asked the bartender what he would do with it. He was told, "Take it, kid; that fight's history." History, indeed! Bob sold that poster for $300.

The International Boxing Hall of Fame in Canastota, New York, has been a prominent venue for exhibiting his vast collection. Some of the many fighters and boxing luminaries that acquired Bob's pristine, crafted memorabilia were Emile Griffith, Joey Giardello, Earnie Shavers, Billy Graham, boxing writer Wally Matthews, and Randy Gordon, former New York State boxing commissioner and editor of *Ring* magazine.

A recipient of notable commendations and honors, Bob was inducted into the New Jersey Boxing Hall of Fame as a boxing historian and received the Sugar Ray Robinson Memorial Award from Ring 25 of the International Veteran Boxers Association (IVBA).

It is with utmost esteem, admiration and respect for our cherished friend, Bob Fernandez, and his unbridled enthusiasm for the sport of boxing—a love that has lasted for over six decades—that we are deeply honored and privileged to introduce the reader to this remarkable record of boxing in New Jersey.

Tommy A. Kaczmarek is a distinguished world boxing judge; World Boxing Council (WBC) chairman, Ring Officials Board; author, You Be the (Boxing) Judge; teacher of global judging seminars; former professional boxer; and member of the New Jersey Boxing Hall of Fame.

Peter R. Nozza is a past president of the International Veteran Boxers Association (IVBA), Ring 25; honored manager and trainer of amateur and professional championship boxers; and member of the New Jersey Boxing Hall of Fame.

2

Preface

My love affair with boxing, the great sport which is also known as the "sweet science," started when I was five years old. It started with me sitting on my dad's knee listening to the radio with the focus on Joe Louis fights. Joe fought often, almost always a knockout winner. I was hooked.

For seventy-five years since, I've read everything I could find on the sport. That covers thousands of magazines and countless newspaper articles of accounts of the fights. As I grew older I enjoyed talking fights with anyone who had knowledge of boxing. They included fighters, trainers, cut men, managers, etc. My favorite were the old-time "gym rats." They were the guys who hung around the gyms endlessly and told little-known stories of the boxing stars of past and present.

This gave me a vast knowledge of boxing which I stored in my memory bank and added to over the many years. I consider this my research for my boxing articles.

Besides haunting the gyms and training camps, I attended hundreds of fights, mostly in New Jersey and New York City. I admired and forged a deep respect for these gladiators. I adored them. Thus the title *Boxing in New Jersey, 1900–1999*. My writings focus on the old-timers, whose memories I hope never fade away.

Their kin and grandchildren will be amazed that they are still remembered and written about. They may also find out just how good and tough "Grandpa" was.

All aspects of boxing, your author tried. Amateur boxing, trainer, sparring partner, memorabilia collector and finally, in my twilight years, writer documenting the sport I love. Some of the stories I wrote were popular, and it led to my induction into the New Jersey Boxing Hall of Fame in 2006.

What follows is a firsthand account of the golden age of New Jersey boxing, from the amateurs to the champions, the trainers, managers and hangers-on, from the aging, rickety fight clubs to venues such as Madison Square Garden. It offers a vivid description of the blood, sweat, tears and ambition of the many boxers who tried to fight their way from poverty and hard times to wealth and respectability. Some made it, and some didn't, but all of them benefitted from the experience. Boxing has a way of turning young bullies into upright citizens, even role models. It teaches them discipline and respect for their opponent, and it has its own way of offering life-lessons to its rough-and-tumble participants.

James J. Braddock:
Cinderella Man

It is only fitting and proper to start with the "leader" of the parade of great New Jersey boxers, the Irish American heavyweight, James J. Braddock. Proud of his heritage, he and his team emphasized the "James J." There was James J. Corbett and James J. Jeffries, and then James J. Braddock—all world heavyweight champions.

Braddock was the last of the James Js. He fought through the Great Depression, and the only luck he ever had was bad luck. That is, until June 1, 1935, the night he became the Cinderella Man and as a 10–1 underdog whipped the lethally hard-punching Max Baer to a 15-round decision win to annex the heavyweight championship of the world—up until then the biggest upset in boxing history. He immediately became known as the Cinderella Man, a man who became the hero of the American people. He gave them confidence and hope that if he could scramble his way out of poverty, then the tens of thousands like him could do it too.

There has been a book and a movie of the same title, *Cinderella Man*, released early in the 21st century to hot and cold reviews. It's my belief that both book and movie were two decades late. It's my impression that to really appreciate both book and movie, one had to live during the Great Depression to understand just how good those works are. Many people who lived through the Depression are now gone.

When old-timers talk about that time, the younger crew thinks they are BSing. They refuse to believe just how hard it is to live in poverty. They can't comprehend that a family, in order to save a few pennies on toilet paper, would use newspapers in its place. They would buy a newspaper for two or three cents, read it all over then put it next to the toilet. Double use.

Members of the family were told that in their daily routine if they came upon any loose wood to bring it home for the kitchen woodstove, it would supply heat for the kitchen (the only room in the flat heated) and also furnish the heat for cooking. They also scrounged large hunks of soft coal that fell off the railroad cars. Chores like this became normal routine to those who lived through the Great Depression.

James J. Braddock knew all this. A married man with a wife and three children, this worn-out "pug" took on any job he could find to supplement his meager earnings from his boxing career, which was slowed down by broken hands. At times his right hand would not be completely healed when he was offered another fight, which he would take because his children were hungry and he was behind with the rent. Result: the hand would be broken again. Finally Jim was completely overwhelmed; this hardworking honest man, a very proud man, had to apply for welfare, which in the Depression era was known as "relief." Jim had hit rock bottom.

In September 1933 Jim retired, truly disgusted with the broken hands that dogged him. He went to work on the Hoboken, New Jersey, docks as a stevedore, lugging freight and cargo off ships. He would "shape up" every morning, hoping to be picked for a day's work. Some days he worked, other days not.

Joe Gould, Jim's manager-trainer, never gave up on Jim's ability. He kept begging promoters to use Jim. They all claimed Jim was a burned-out fighter—a has been. Gould persisted and finally obtained a match for Jim against the red-hot prospect Corn Griffin. With only three days' notice, Braddock left the docks and fought Griffin, who was heavily favored.

Griffin blasted Jim to the canvas in the first round. Jim struggled to finish the round. He knew he had to win this fight to stay marketable with the promoters and continue to get meaningful fights. He called on all his resolve to come back, and that he did with one booming right hand in the third round to win by knockout. Even Jim and Joe Gould did not realize that the months Jim was away from the ring gave his right hand time to heal properly. What an upset! This was the turning point of Braddock's career, the first step leading up to the greatest come-back in heavyweight history. This fight earned Jim two more fights, and he was able to upset John Henry Lewis and Art Lasky. These wins got him a title shot at the Big Bad Baer, the heavyweight champion many believed was the hardest-hitting right-hand puncher of all the former champs, from the great John L. Sullivan up. It would be Max Baer's first title defense. No one, even Braddock's most ardent fans, gave Jim a chance. Most fans thought Jim was a lamb being led to slaughter.

Max Baer was known to have caused the death of two men in the squared circle with that deadly right cross. Baer was known as the "glamour boy of the ring." He had the best build of heavyweight champions before him. He had the body beautiful. The women were crazy about him. He was as handsome as any movie star, and Hollywood used him in movies. Baer could have been an all-time heavyweight great but threw it all away. He preferred being the "clown." He was also called the "clown prince of sock." Yes, he also was a notorious womanizer; his manager and trainer had a hell of a time trying to keep him in training camp. Against Braddock he had every advantage—youth, size, power and a champion's confidence in himself. He figured he would take Braddock out in five rounds or less.

Braddock had a pleasing stand-up style, sort of like the English heavyweights. He had a good left jab and hook. He could box fairly well and had a crisp right cross; a right cross that at one time was feared by all light heavyweight challengers. That was the division Braddock started in, but that right hand was broken a number of times. When he moved up to the heavyweight division, his big right was a much lesser threat. In training camp Braddock was working hard, and he felt his right was better than ever. Max was playing the buffoon with his spar mates and his audience of fans and press personnel. Always the clown.

As the first-round bell faded away, Baer found out Braddock had absolutely no fear of him. Braddock took charge, sticking a neat left jab into Max's face. That was Jim's modus operandi, to jab, move and throw straight right hands to head and body, always moving away from Baer's vaunted right-hand bomb. Braddock got off to a good lead. By the fifth round Baer finally got the message. This guy was for real. He had come to take Max's title. Max stopped playing to the audience and got serious. He started throwing haymakers in desperation and forced Braddock into heated exchanges. Jim was ready for this and often outslugged Max in these exchanges. Jim knew he had to be extremely careful with the deadly punching of an aroused Baer.

In the sixth round Baer found himself tiring. He now regretted the nights he sneaked out of training camp to go to the city for fun and games. Braddock was fresh, and he sensed Max being tired. Baer was getting sloppy with his punching, leaving himself wide open for Braddock combinations. All Jim had to do now was keep circling away from Baer's right hand and pepper him good. Jim Braddock won a well-deserved 15-round decision and the biggest prize in all of sports: the Heavyweight Championship of the World. Daymon Runyan dubbed him the "Cinderella Man," and Braddock became an instant folk hero.

The world of boxing was stunned. The New Jersey underdog contender had defeated a young, in-his-prime champion, the murderous puncher Max Baer. Everyone had laughed at James J. Braddock and his loyal-beyond-belief manager Joe Gould. Joe loved Braddock like his own son. He pulled off a business deal with Mike Jacobs, the slick boxing promoter, that is still talked about and remembered to this very day. I believe Gould did this as his tribute to Braddock. They could laugh at him, but Joe Gould outfoxed the fox himself, Mike Jacobs.

Jacobs had that great young contender, the "Brown Bomber" out of Detroit, under contract: Joe Louis. He had wiped out the heavyweight division, flattening all comers. Max Baer, just three months after losing his title to Braddock, took on Louis and was knocked out in four rounds, an easy win for the dark destroyer. Gould knew that Braddock as new champion would have to defend the title against the number-one challenger, which of course was Joe Louis. Gould and Braddock both knew that Jim had no chance against the Brown Bomber, no chance at all. Gould made promoter Jacobs and his tiger wait two years before he would sign for the fight. Jacobs was desperate; he wanted control of the heavyweight championship. With a Louis victory, he would have the champ under contract for all his future fights.

Joe Gould made him pay. The fight would be sealed only after Jacobs agreed to pay Gould and Braddock 10 percent of Jacobs' profits from each title defense Louis would make. Jacobs was in between a rock and a hard place. He had no choice but to agree. What a bonanza it turned out to be. Louis of course won that title and went on to defend his title *25 times*, a heavyweight title record which will probably never be broken. He kept the championship for eleven and a half years.

Braddock and Gould milked all they could get out of the title, and who could blame them? They made professional appearances, speaking engagements, commercial ads and any way they could make a buck while still champion. That was the two years between the Baer and Louis fights. Jacobs was going bonkers from the long wait. He also had to agree that Braddock as champ got the lion's share of the Braddock vs. Louis purse.

In June of 1937 Braddock and Louis finally met. Jim gave his fans a ray of hope when he surprisingly dropped the Brown Bomber for a short count in the very first round. But that ray of hope was quickly extinguished when Louis started connecting with his vicious punching. Braddock took a terrible beating until he was counted out in the eighth round. Other fighters would have quit long before the eighth from such a beating, but Braddock wanted to go out like a champion—on his shield. Since Dempsey slaughtered Jess Willard, no heavyweight champion had shown such grit and gameness in a desperate attempt to retain that title as Braddock. It was Jim's belief, "If you want that title, you have to kill me to get it." Louis almost did just that. Jim's face was a mass of cuts. Mike Jacobs got his champion; Louis went on to be one of the greatest ever. Braddock would fight one more time and retire to his beloved North Bergen, New Jersey, home that he bought after the Baer victory. He died in that home November 30, 1974. He was a very popular champion, and a credit to boxing.

I had the privilege of meeting Jim in the early 1960s at a Golden Glove show in my hometown, Elizabeth, New Jersey. He was introduced to the audience, and the mayor of the town presented him with the key to the city, a large gold-colored key probably made of wood. After a standing ovation, Jim said only a few words to the crowd and proceeded down the ring steps. I made it my business to be there waiting at the bottom of the steps. I shook his hand and congratulated him. He smiled and said, "I wish this key was the key to the city bank," and we both laughed.

From the time I was a kid, I always wished I would one day shake hands with a heavyweight champion. Wishes do come true. Old-timers in the days of John L. Sullivan used to brag if they had met Sullivan and tell their friends, "Shake the hand that shook the hand of the great John L."

That incident is one of the many fond ones that I keep in my memory.

Boxing Spawns Gentlemen:
An Ode to Vic Creelman

There was an episode in my life that I will never forget. Even though some may think it is trivial and of little consequence, to me it was an absorbing lesson on building character while gaining respect for your fellow man.

It was in the early 1960s. The place was Woyt's Tavern, at the corner of Stiles Street and Elizabeth Avenue, Linden, New Jersey; it was a very popular pub and grill frequented by the employees of the many large factories and small plants in the area.

After working in a meat warehouse all day I always looked forward to stopping at Woyt's for my usual Bratwurst sandwich (the best in town) and my tall glass of cold beer. The afternoon the incident happened I was a little late getting to the bar. My crew was already there and the place was standing room only. Woyt's business was humongous at the end of the day shift six days a week. When I walked in and worked my way through the crowd to the bar, I saw the reason for the extra chatter and laughter.

There was a little man in a business suit holding court among the huge crowd of blue-collar workers. They were hanging on to every word he uttered. I asked one of my fellow workers, "Who is this guy and what's he selling?" "Beer, he's selling beer. He's an ex-pug and a liquor salesman for a big company. His name is Vic Creelman." I had heard of him. He used to fight in the New York City clubs.

Creelman was holding a clinic on Willie Pep, the former great featherweight champion. Vic had challenged the crowd that if they could answer his questions on Pep, for each correct answer he would buy a round of drinks. So far the customers had gotten only one right: Willie

Pep was Italian-American. Drink up, men. Creelman continued with a tougher question. Who did Pep win the title from? Everyone was quiet. I then blurted out, "Chalky Wright." Vic feigned huge surprise and said, "Well, well, we have an 'expert' in our midst." I was embarrassed as everyone cheered and Creelman came over to me and introduced himself. He was surprised that I had heard of him as his fighting days were long over. He challenged me to answer more of his questions, giving me the feeling he was slightly PO'd. After all, I did steal his captive audience. Some of the guys I worked with told Creelman he was making a mistake, for they knew I was pretty well up on my study of pugilism.

Vic then said, "Okay, expert, try this one. Who did Chalky Wright win the title from?" With no hesitation I gave him "Joey Archibald." Creelman was visibly stunned. Another round of beer and the cheering was deafening. It created an atmosphere of a serious contest. The guys started mocking Creelman; he laughed it off, but one could see it was bothering him. Next question, "Who was the first man to defeat the undefeated Willie Pep and what number was his streak halted at?" Sammy Angott—sixty-three. Again Vic threw up his hands in mock disbelief. I had just taken him for three rounds of drinks. The crowd had got him for one before I arrived, so that made it four. Vic then said, "Okay, expert, you may know a lot about Willie Pep; let's see what you can do with Joe Louis. He defended his heavyweight title twenty-five times. Who was his first challenger and what round did he stop him in?" "Welshman Tommy Farr. Louis did not stop him; he won a 15-round decision." Cheers with laughter at Creelman. Vic was trying to defend his reputation as a well-versed historian of the sweet science in local bars. I found this out from the bartender later on.

Vic insisted on one more question. I told him he was losing money and I did not want to be the cause. To my surprise he explained that as a salesman he was allowed to buy so many free rounds for the customers in the bars he serviced. His company, I believe, was Pabst Blue Ribbon; they footed the bill and racked it up as advertisement. I agreed to a burst of cheers. The men set this one up by calling Creelman, "chicken, chicken, you're afraid of him." By this time we all had drunk five beers free, bought by Vic's company. My shoulders were sore from getting slapped on them by men congratulating me on each correct answer. Everyone was getting a little sloppy. It happens when you drink beer fast.

Creelman wasn't drinking, and he came up with a good one on his next question. Back to the featherweights. "Who did Joey Archibald win the title from?" I knew the answer, but for the life of me I couldn't think of his name at that moment. With everyone looking at me and waiting for the correct answer, I blurted out a fighter's name of that era, Leo Rodak. I was wrong and I knew it.

To my astonishment Creelman said, "He did it again." I looked at him straight in the eye; we both knew I was wrong. Vic told the bartender to set up the round. All my buddies were slapping me on the back and continued to mock Creelman, who told them, "That's it, no more questions." He then headed for the men's room. I followed him to find out what in the hell was going on.

Vic confided to me that he had no desire to ruin the fun of such a happy group. He also admired the faith the men had in me for my knowledge of boxing, and he wanted to keep it that way. To Vic it was a great afternoon of boxing front and center. That doesn't happen often. He told me to also cherish the moment and always support boxing. Also never discredit a man in front of his friends. Vic thought he might just do that by correcting me.

This man Creelman was a real gentleman and a true lover of boxing. It was the only meeting I ever had with him, but he left his mark.

On my way home that evening I wondered where I had heard that kind of wisdom before. It finally came to me. The U.S. Navy. When we seamen passed the test for third-class petty officer (the Crow), the officer of the day gave a speech. "Now that you men will be in charge of and giving orders to others, remember one important thing: never chew out, or belittle or degrade a man in front of his peers and friends. Do not steal his thunder. It would be the worst thing you could ever do. You will lose respect. Take him on the side in private and tell him his mistake or what he's done wrong." I then wondered if Vic Creelman was ever in the Navy.

When I returned to the bar the next day, the barkeep told me everyone did well that afternoon. Creelman got the customers to drink Pabst Blue Ribbon, and many stayed till late evening, thereby filling the cash register. I thought, hell, I also was kept undefeated. But many wives in the area opened their front door that evening only to find their husbands standing there inebriated.

When checking up on Vic Creelman's record, the year 1943 was his best. He fought 16 times, losing only one decision. He boxed men like Rocco Rossano, Ruby Kessler, Aaron Perry, Cleo Shans and Charley Riley; old-timers will remember them. I do not know if Vic is still with us, but the fact remains he did lose five rounds at Woyt's Tavern. He is one of those special people that you may only meet once in a lifetime but never forget them. By the way, the answer to the question "Who did Joey Archibald win the title from?" was Harry Jeffra.

The Jersey Nightstick:
Tony Galento and
Other Jersey Bombers

New Jersey has long been known as a hotbed of boxing. From the days when the state was dotted with small fight clubs, to the ball parks, Roosevelt and Ruppert Stadiums. There was Meadowbrook and Twin City Bowls, along with the Armories, Newark, Jersey City, and Elizabeth with Laurel Garden in Newark. All are now gone from the fistic scene. As far back as the early 1920s when Jersey City hosted the first million-dollar gate in boxing history with the Jack Dempsey–Georges Carpentier fight, the arena on Boyles' Thirty Acres held 50,000 people and was expanded to hold up to 93,000 just for that heavyweight title fight. It was on July 2, 1921, a sold-out packed house, plus over 700 reporters from all over the world. Those were the rabid fight fans of New Jersey. It went that way until the early 1950s when TV started putting on fights six nights a week. The fans started staying home and watched the fights for free.

Boxing carried on, though, and the casinos of Atlantic City picked up the slack. The casino owners knew that the fights would draw in customers, fight fans who before and after watching the bouts would give the gambling tables a shot. Promoting fights in Atlantic City reached a high pitch for some time and slowly leveled off to what we have today.

How could New Jersey not have spawned some of the greatest fighters the world has known? The state boasts two heavyweight champions, the "real undisputed lineal" type of years ago, they being James J. Braddock and Jersey Joe Walcott. Ironically, both came off the relief, or as they say today, welfare rolls—hungry enough to battle their way to gold and glory. Other Jersey "undisputed real champs" included the great

14

Mickey Walker and Freddie Cochrane, Ike Williams, Tippy Larkin, as well as Gus Lesnivich, Vince and Johnny Dundee, Johnny Buff and Willie La Morte. Other champs came later, but they were not the original lineal—top contenders such as Ernie Schaaf, Steve Dudas, Charley Fusari, Ernie Durando, Allie Stolz, and Freddy Archer down to and not forgetting "the Bayonne Bleeder" and warrior personified Chuck Wepner, and many more, too numerous to mention. New Jersey produced the best, promoters, trainers, managers, referees, etc. Former fighter Paul Cavilier did one of the best ref jobs this writer ever saw when he refereed the third Graziano-Zale fight. It was total and complete, no second guesses; with early stoppages Paul counted out a flattened Rocky in round three. Rocky never stirred, but Paul finished the ten count. Other standout refs recalled are former heavyweight contender Randy Neumann, Tony Orlando, Jr., and Larry Hazzard, among so many others. In promoters, standouts were George Kobb, Lou Duva, the Bozza brothers, etc. Managers Bill Daly, Willie Gilzenberg, and Angelo Pucci come to mind. The best and most famous of all boxing judges, Tommy Kaczmarek, started as a nifty boxing featherweight with an iron jaw who completed his career a winning one. Never had a "soft" opponent and never heard the ten count—quite a resume for the Elizabeth native. One would not believe by looking at him that he was a pugilist—he's unmarked.

Yet there was one fighter who stood out, a fighter who never won a championship yet became a household name from his performance in one certain fight. That man was Two-Ton Tony Galento, the Orange, New Jersey, Nightstick. He didn't look like a fighter, and couldn't box very well, but still he became famous the world over.

Two-Ton Tony was born Dominick Anthony Galento, March 12, 1910, in Orange, New Jersey, of Italian parentage. Times were tough, and growing up, so was Tony. He quit school early for the simple reason that he hated it. He wanted to go to work and make some money. Tony took on some hard jobs in which he met manual labor. Manny was a real badass. Tony didn't hit it off well with labor, so he decided to disassociate himself with Manny. Tony at the time was hanging around the local gyms. He weighed around 160 and started to spar with the local pugs. Tony had a rough-and-tumble style and held his own well with some of the experienced spar mates. He knew that a winning fighter even in the prelims made more money in one night than he did in a month working with Mr. Labor. He made up his mind; this is what he would do. He started his pro career in 1928, weighing in around 165 and standing 5'9" tall. By 1929 Tony was weighing in at 200; his opponents were now heavyweights. He was too short to be any kind of boxer, so it was a slam-bang charge-in style he used. The weight Tony put on was due to his love of pasta and beer. He also loved to smoke them big cigars. Training, he could take it or leave it. He was getting plenty of fights, winning most, and making money, so who really has to train that hard? That was Tony's philosophy. Tony could always punch very hard with his left hook, and he perfected it to almost a lethal weapon. All his fights held high drama. The opponent and fans never knew when that left hook would put the lights out. Fighters would outbox Tony, but they knew one mistake and it could be curtains. Tony's services were in demand even though by relying on the left hook he sometimes would lose by decision. Some nights the left hook just didn't land.

Tony got married to his childhood sweetheart and later bought a bar, in of all places, Orange, New Jersey. The left hook was landing often, with more accuracy.

The boxing writers of the day started calling Tony's left hook the Orange, New Jersey, Nightstick, referring to a policeman's club. And what a club it was. Tony was scoring strings of knockouts. The same writers called Tony other names—none too flattering. One was "Two-Ton," because of his obesity. They delighted in calling him "Baboon," "Beer Barrel," "Beer Keg with Legs," or the "Orange Orangutan." The only name they got right was the Nightstick.

Galento had many managers early on, but things started to gel when he took on the legendary Joe Jacobs. Jacobs was the man who was probably responsible for Max Schmeling winning the Heavyweight Championship of the World in a fight with Jack Sharkey, the winner to take the crown left vacated by Gene Tunny. Sharkey sunk one low, and Schmeling hit the deck. With coaching from Jacobs, Max was able to put on a gigantic act of pain, and along with Jacobs screaming "foul" at the top of his lungs, it brought forth the first time in boxing history a fighter won the heavyweight title on a foul. To this day it still stands. So Jacobs positively could move Galento to the top. The man was a ballyhoo wizard.

Joe Louis was heavyweight champion. His promoter and managers knew World War II was coming; Hitler was on the move in Europe. They agreed that Joe would and should fight often in order to make them all rich. They knew Joe was at his peak; the competition would do him good. They would take all the fights they could before the war and Uncle Sam got hold of Joe. They would need challengers.

Galento's manager Jacobs could figure this out. Jacobs started matching Tony with fighters who fought Louis. Then he would try to get Two-Ton to better Joe's time of kayo. Of the six common opponents, Galento also knocked them all out, matching Louis's round twice and bettering it once.

Things like this got people to take notice. Jacobs had the writers and the fans comparing the two fighters; he knew this would lead to a title shot for Tony. He was right.

Jacobs figured he must build up Tony all he could. People were thinking Joe Louis was unbeatable, a living legend. In those days there was no TV money, so to make money you had to get the butts in the seats at the stadium. The press was the only way to go. The fight fans had to know more of Galento. The boxing writers knew Tony was one of a kind, a misfit because he just didn't look like a heavyweight challenger should. Fat and bold and hairy, he looked more like a wrestler. He didn't train like a fighter. He smoked cigars and guzzled beer, which top contenders are not supposed to do. He was a character, probably the most boisterous since the days of John L. Sullivan, when that strong boy would pound his fist on the local bar and yell that he "could knock out any SOB in the house." Tony owned a bar, and when the Louis bout started to lean into reality, Tony would bang his fist on the bar and growl, "I'll moider da bum," with his thick New Joicey accent, just like John L. Sullivan used to do with his Boston accent. Joe Jacobs liked what he saw and encouraged Tony, telling him that was the way to sell tickets. Jacobs had the newspapers take photos of Tony downing full pitchers of beer, smoking cigars while punching the bag, and carrying kegs of beer to "enhance his training," all the while repeating "I'll moider da bum." He had a gym in back of his bar. For the newsmen he would spar with some of his drinking buddies, throwing only left hooks. It was great copy; people were reading Galento and started thinking maybe that Nightstick could do the job. Galento looked and sounded like a Damon Runyon character. Joe Jacobs made him even more so. Tony was now good copy. On the way up, Tony lost a few fights by disqualification; he would throw punches from all angles, some south of the border. He'd use his head because he was always in with a taller opponent. And Tony enjoyed fighting viciously. Once the bell rang, Tony was out to win any way he could. The boxing writers called him a "dirty fighter." Galento's reply and famous quote: "They call me a doity fighter. Hell, I train hard, I drink plenty of beer, smoke cigars and take three showers a day, and dose news guy bums call me doity. Da bums."

The Louis-Galento fight was finally signed. Louis's team knew Galento had a punch equal to the hardest-hitting heavyweights up to that time, they being Dempsey, Louis and Max Baer. They had a punch with boxing ability to go with it. Galento had a left hook and a walk-in roughhouse style; he could take a good shot, and that was it. His defense was simply stopping blows with his face. They figured Louis had nothing to worry about. Tony had eleven straight KOs going into the Louis fight. Yet the boxing writers called it a gross mismatch, thus hurting the gate. Louis was an 8–1 favorite. There was hardly any betting on the fight. As the fight drew near, the writers must have forgotten the Nightstick. Tony weighed in at 233¾ and Louis 200¾. Held at Yankee Stadium on June 28, 1939, the attendance was 34,852, which grossed $333,308. Louis's share was $96,323; Two-Ton's, $42,141—all figures taken from the next day's sport pages. For Tony he would generate money from the fight for years to come.

As Mills Lane would say, "Let's get it on." Round one, Louis admitted he figured he would toy with the funny-looking bald fat man for a few rounds before administering the knockout drops. He had heard of Tony's left hook, but he was feeling cocky; no way was this fat guy going to land on him. They sparred around with Joe sticking out that beautiful jab of his finding Tony's face. Galento showed no fear of Joe, piling into him with bull strength. Then it happened—a nightstick left hook staggered Louis. He was hurt bad, as he would later admit. Joe grabbed a rushing-in Galento and held on for dear life. He used all his skills to finish the round with Tony in pursuit. He blamed himself for taking Two-Ton so lightly.

Joe settled down in the second, cutting both Galento's eyes and telling himself that after the first-round "shockwaves," he'd better get rid of this funny-looking man ASAP. Louis started looking to land his kayo punch in the third but got careless by dropping his right, and zap it landed again. Joe was *down*. Tony had landed the nightstick again. Joe was up at once, a hurt fighter. Galento stormed in, but Joe was able to recover. Louis put out an all assault in the fourth, an avalanche of blows to get this fat guy out of there. Galento was punched into a bleeding hulk, stopped at 2:29 of the fourth round. Referee Arthur Donovan humanely halted the fight. Galento was a hero in defeat; the stadium had rocked in the third round when Joe hit the deck. It was one hell of a fight for as long as it lasted. Some writers called it the best heavyweight brawl in 16 years, since Dempsey-Firpo went berserk at the Polo Grounds.

Orange, New Jersey, hailed Tony as its hero. Over 7,500 Galento fans surrounded the bistro owned by Tony. Every car that had a radio was tuned in to the fight. Traffic was at a standstill for blocks around Two-Ton's saloon. Fans that brought their own backed up the one radio at the bar. When Louis was floored, all bedlam broke loose. When ref Donovan stopped the fight, boos drowned out the broadcast. They calmed down when Tony spoke from ringside. Then the fans waited four hours until Tony appeared at his club and gave him a thunderous ovation.

Some excerpts taken from the paper the next day were all Galento. Murray Robinson, who wrote a column *Calling the Turn*, entitled it "The Gallant Goff," expressing these opinions: A victor in defeat. He is now world famous. Galento needed no alibis for his friends. He thought he let them down. His trainer and his manager decided on a strategy that would confuse Joe. They told Tony to stay in a crouch and stay covered up until inside of Joe's left, then start swinging. As long as Tony stayed in that position, he did fine. From that position he landed those terrific nightstick hooks in the first and third rounds. Tony failed to stick to that strategy. He straightened up, and as soon as he did his finish was written in gore. Johnny Dundee, the old champ, pointed out that Galento had to come up out of his crouch because it was exhausting for him to remain in that position for any length of time. "Try it sometime," suggested Johnny, "and see how you feel. And you'd feel worse if you had a shape like Galento." Not a bad tactic. Louis would have fits against another crouch, Arturo Godoy, seven months later, winning a split 15-round decision. In the stifling Yankee Stadium dressing room, the

Gallant Goff sat there, shoulders sagging, muttering needless alibis while the airwaves and telegraph wires were singing his praises around the world as the hero of the fight won by the Brown Bomber.

Galento's trainer Jimmy Frain claimed that Two-Ton lost his golden opportunity to dethrone Louis in the third round by pulling a glaring novice's boner. Tony dropped Louis with the nightstick hook. He was so sure that Joe was down for a long stay that he turned his back on him to walk to the far corner, as per the rules. When he turned around again, he found that Louis had bounced to his feet almost at one. The few seconds' rest Joe got from Tony's trip to the neutral corner and back was enough to allow him to recuperate.

"If Tony had only backed away from Louis, he'd be champion. He would have seen the befuddled champ bounce right up, badly hurt, and he could have swarmed all over him—a cinch to knock him dead before he could regain his bearings."

As for Louis, his right cheek cut and bruised from Galento's fists in the first round, he admitted that the Orange barkeep had given him his toughest fight of his career. Tony was Joe's seventh title defense.

Tony's opinion was "if dey (his trainer and manager) had let me fight my fight, I would have moidered da bum. Never again. They told me to crouch, keep covered up and fight a sissy fight. I did that and what did it get me? Knocked out. I wanted to fight my regular fight, rough, and maul him from the start, but they wouldn't let me. I'm sure I would have won if they had let me alone."

Of course Tony screamed for a return bout. John Roxborough and Julian Black, Louis's co-managers, turned it down. They never fought again. It is said Galento was the only challenger Louis disliked. Being the sensitive man he was, he never relished Tony constantly calling him a bum. That's the only time Tony's big mouth got in his way, scuttling a Louis return match.

Louis was a great fighter, a great champion. People of that day figured Joe to be unbeatable, thus the clamor of Galento's great feat of putting him on the deck. My memory of the Louis fights on the radio were, and I recall vividly, sitting on my dad's knee listening to that large radio. It was as big as me. My dad listened to all the fights, and I'd join him. I recall asking him after another Louis victory if Superman or Batman could beat Louis. His reply was no, but a fellow named "Father Time" would. I didn't understand what he meant at the time, and he didn't elaborate, Dad being a man of few words. I found out about ten years later when Ezzard Charles and Rocky Marciano beat Louis just what my dad meant. Joe Louis was a true hero of the blue-collar working class. Other heroes names I heard from that big radio were Henry Armstrong, Fritzi Zivic, Gus Lesnivick, Billy Conn, Fred Apostali and of course Willie Pep and Sugar Ray Robinson among others. I didn't know what they looked like until my older brother showed me the sports pages. In those days the papers actually printed photos of boxers in their fighting poses. They also had "last night's fight results" from all over the country—oh the good old days. Fighters got "ink" and fans could read about them.

In Galento's next fight, just 79 days after the Louis encounter, he would meet the up-and-coming Lou Nova, a fine fighter who was a standout amateur and now going great guns as a heavyweight contender. Many boxing writers and fans claim this fight was the most brutal and bloodiest heavyweight fight ever. Both Galento and Nova were covered with gore, as was the blood-spattered referee. The front of his shirt carried the "Red Badge of Courage." Galento was at his dirty-fighting best on this night. He used his head as a battering ram, his thumbs to gouge Nova's eyes, and the laces of his gloves to rake Nova's face. Also his knee he positioned into Lou's groin. Rabbit punches, kidney punches, and low blows were followed by verbal abuse. That was Galento's greeting to Nova who entered the ring a clean-cut young heavyweight. He would be kayoed in the 14th round. He was a battered bleeding wreck when he left the ring. He learned a lesson he would never forget about dirty fighting. Lou was a novice in foul fighting, and when Galento started it early, Nova had to defend himself, so he tried to return Galento's favors. Big mistake. He was up against a master of foul tactics. The referee warned them both early, but the fouls continued. It was said the ref, George Blake, after many warnings told the fighters, "If that's the way you want it, so be it." That was all Galento had to hear. In the end both fighters had to be hospitalized. Nova said many times then, and in later years, that he never spoke to Galento again, although their paths crossed many times at boxing functions and affairs.

Nova was a young man taken to school by a man who had no scruples once the bell rang. Many people believed Nova was ruined in that fight, although he did go on to challenge Joe Louis for the title. It was said he could have been a better fighter had he not fought Tony Galento. Tony's beating took something out of Nova. He was never the same and never developed into the fighter he was expected to be. I cannot fathom why a young, hard-hitting fighter, a fine prospect such as Nova, was put in there at that time of his promising career with the rampaging Orange Orangutan.

In Galento's next two fights, he would run into two Baers, Max and Buddy. The Baer brothers, Max, the former heavyweight champion of the world who was one of the hardest punchers in boxing history, and his big little brother Buddy who could hit like hell. Max could have been an all-time great, but he preferred being a playboy and a clown. He wasted his career. Galento really wanted no part of Max, and he made no bones about it to his manager Joe Jacobs. Jacobs made the match anyway. Tony knew Max could really bang and could box well if he so desired. Tony also knew Baer's punch had killed one fighter, Frankie Campbell, and was indirectly responsible for another's death. Tony knew it was a no-win match for him. Galento was brave, but he was badly battered and couldn't answer the eighth round bell. Nine months later the younger but bigger Baer made Galento a seventh round kayo victim. That finished Galento as a big-time fighter. Joe Jacobs died before the first Baer fight, and Willie Gilzenberg took over Galento's management. "Gilly" would milk the Galento-Louis fight for years to come. After all, it had made Galento a hero and a household name. Galento would be able to and did make money the rest of his life from the fame he won for himself from that one fight, along with some good old-fashioned ballyhoo and hype from some very crafty promoters. These men often made up stories of Tony's prowess, having Galento pose for all sorts of gimmick photos for the press. It was Gilly who started Two-Ton on a career as a wrestler. He also matched him with kangaroos, bears, and even an octopus and anything else he could think of. It was reported that Galento, who fought the giant squid in the front window of a large California fish market, won the decision. The squid died three days later. With all these novelty "fights," Galento was riding high, high enough for Gilly to get Tony many guest referee spots, greeter jobs, speaking engagements, and TV and movie bit parts. Of all these stories told about Galento, whether fabricated or true, this one stands out and is expected to be the truth for no other reason than that the promoter never told it. None other than "the Great One," Jackie Gleason, told the tale, on a TV talk show many years ago. Jackie was at his peak then, a multimillionaire, so there was no reason why he should make the story up. No one could believe the story was bogus, especially with Jackie getting the short end of the "stick."

The yarn goes like this: Jackie was on hard times, a struggling comedian out of work. He jumped at a chance offered to him to work a weekend at a well-known rowdy nightspot in Newark, New Jersey. Jackie had worked many "tough spots" before, and he would handle it. He was flat broke and needed the bread. Gleason came out and got off a few good one-liners. He immediately had the crowd in stitches. All but one person, that is; this portly, bald beer guzzler with the cigar in his face kept harassing Gleason. Every joke Jackie got off, the rowdy patron had a remark for. Jackie struggled on, but the fat guy kept calling him a bum and other choice names. Jackie got so frustrated he started throwing insults back at the intruder in an effort to shame him into shutting up. Jackie finally told the guy to leave—still no go. The man kept up his tirade until Gleason blurted out, "Look, Buddy, I'll see you in the alley after the show." Now Gleason, when it came to fisticuffs, was no slouch; he was known to be able to take care of himself. Gleason would never turn down a fight when provoked. He always did well in roughhouse and had confidence in himself.

Jackie stepped out in the alley and confronted "baldy" in his best pugilistic pose. That was all he remembers. The nightstick had landed. It was Jackie Gleason who "went to the moon," long before Alice ever did. When his faithful cronies were finally able to bring Gleason back to the living, he moaned, "Who the hell was that?" A witness to that one-punch kayo claimed, "That was a local pug name of Tony Galento; he fights the small clubs around here." So Jackie Gleason felt the thunder that was the nightstick long before Joe Louis would get the chance.

One night while attending a fight at the Newark Armory, years after Tony had retired, we had the pleasure of seeing Two-Ton again. My friends and I were in our usual spot, the balcony with the rest of the gallery rats. We looked down on the arena floor, and there standing behind the last row of seats directly below us was Two-Ton holding court with his friends. This area was always the hangout place for "the boys," sort of a gathering of fighters, trainers, managers and hard-core fans who would shoot the breeze during the fights. Tony had the floor and was preaching boxing to those around him, his hands gesturing wildly. I noticed that each man who would talk directly to Tony would first put his hands on Two-Ton's shoulders and then in a very friendly way drop his hands down the length of Tony's arms and then pin Tony's arms to the sides of his legs, there by rendering Tony's left hook useless. These guys knew that Tony was a little punchy, and when excited he was known to shadowbox a hit. We were cracking up watching Tony and his buddies and missing the good prelim action in the ring. After all these years people still feared that mighty nightstick.

Tony did a lot of work in Hollywood, getting small cameo parts in quite a few movies. His best role was in the Academy Award–winning picture *On the Waterfront*. It starred Marlon Brando, and Tony portrayed "Truck," a union strong arm. Tony didn't have to act; he was a truck, and Hollywood pegged him right. Other fighters in the movie were Abe Simon, Tami Mauriello and Lee Oma, quite a rugged crew for hero Marlon Brando to tame.

Yes, Two-Ton Tony Galento was a one-of-a-kind character boxing will never forget. Tony died July 22, 1979, at age 69 of a heart attack. Diabetes had taken both of his legs before then. Tony fought for 17 years and had over 100 fights, winning over 50 by knockout. He called all fighters "bums"; he also called all persons he liked "bums." Also, Tony outside the ring was a great big loveable teddy bear.

Ike Williams: Lightweight Champion Extraordinaire

In the past 65 years I've seen many great lightweight champions and contenders, either on TV, film, tape or in the flesh. The two greatest I believe were New Jerseyite Ike Williams and Panama's Roberto Duran. Having never seen Benny Leonard, Joe Gans or Tony Canzaneri, I omit them. As a lightweight, Duran seemed indestructible. Yet if he and Ike were matched while in their prime, I'd be forced to pick Ike Williams to come out on top in a terrific struggle. A real dream match. I believe it would be very close, with Ike taking a split decision. Ike's boxing and machine-gun combinations would be the difference in a slam-bang affair. If the reader ever caught *ESPN Boxing Classics*, he could see Ike fighting the great Beau Jack in a title match. The fight comes to a conclusion with Williams pinning Jack into a corner and wailing away. In a final combination clip of about 25 well-directed punches, Ike stopped and stepped back from the collapsing Beau Jack. He turned and looked at the referee, giving the ref a chance to stop the fight. It was an act of respect and mercy for a fellow gladiator. The referee did nothing, so being the pro that he was, Williams had to finish the job. Another salvo of shots was landed before the ref acted and called a halt. Beau Jack was brave but finished, his title hopes dashed. It was the first time Beau was TKOed in over 105 fights, discounting the loss to Tony Janiro when Beau dislocated his kneecap. Ike Williams was at his very best, his peak in a career that covered 15 years.

Ike was born August 2, 1923, in Brunswick, Georgia. As a young boy his family moved north to Trenton, New Jersey, in a search for better-paying jobs. He would stay a Trentonite the rest of his life. Williams started his simon-pure career at the tender age of 15, winning many titles in the Trenton-Philadelphia area. He turned pro March 15, 1940, with a four-round decision win over Carmine Fatta. No soft touch was Fatta. Ike was never fed any soft opposition. In his first 15 fights, Williams won ten, five by kayo, lost four decisions and got one draw. In only his eighth fight he was fighting eight-rounders. In the 15th fight he met the more experienced Freddy Archer, a Newark native who already had 30 fights on his resume. Archer, a very good boxer, won the eight-rounder. The loss must have done Williams good and motivated him to run off 33 straight wins. Eighteen of those wins were fought in 1943. On January 25, 1944, the streak was ended. Ike's bitter rival Bob Montgomery kayoed Ike in the 12th round, the "Bob Cat" winning all the way. Ike came back with another win streak, ending when he met up with Willie Joyce, a real tough cookie who would be Ike's pain in the rear his whole career. Every fighter seems to have an opponent who will give him mucho trouble. In Ike's case that fighter was Willie Joyce. They would fight four times, and Ike was able to win once. Joyce had the style to throw Ike off stride. It's happened to all great fighters. Even the undefeated Rocky Marciano had his jinx with an overstuffed light heavy who was able to stay ten rounds with Rocky not once but twice. The man was Tiger Ted Lowry. Rocky admitted that if he fought the Tiger one hundred times he could not kayo him. The Tiger simply took Rocky out of his rhythm. Jack Dempsey fought Fat Willie Meehan four times and could only get one win, two draws and a loss. Meehan and Tiger Ted Lowry remained mediocre throughout their careers, where Willie Joyce was a top-notcher. The third and rubber match with Joyce was held at Madison Square Garden. In a rousing fight, *Ring* magazine picked the 12th and final round as the round of the year for 1945. Joyce was now 2–1 over Williams but their fights were such crowd-pleasers, so closely fought, the demand was in for a fourth fight. And *again* Joyce was the winner in a bruising fight, Joyce getting off the floor in the tenth and final round to cop a split decision.

The fight before the fourth and last Joyce bout, Ike was able to win the NBA version of the World Lightweight Championship by kayoing Juan Zurita of Mexico in Mexico City, a two-round stoppage. The lightweight division was in chaos for years with the National Boxing Association going against the New York State Commission. From 1925 until 1947 each had their own champs, therefore splitting the championship.

Ike Williams would change all that in 1947. He would defend his National Boxing Association (NBA) title against Enrique Bolanos and then Ronnie James the English Empire champion. Ike kayoed them both. The James fight strengthened Ike's claim to the undisputed championship as far as Europe was concerned. Seven fights later on August 4, 1947, Ike hit the motherlode. Not only would he be fighting for the undisputed title, but also he could get revenge for his kayo loss to Bobcat Bob Montgomery. Ike annihilated Montgomery in Philadelphia with a sixth-round kayo. He was the man now. Revenge is sweet, especially if you and your opponent hate each other.

It was typical of Ike to fight often and against stiff opposition. In two fights before his unification title fight with Bob Montgomery, Ike would face two top-rated welterweights, the first a kayo win over Juste Fontaine in late May of 1947. He followed that three weeks later by kayoing Tippy Larkin, the junior welterweight champ, in a non-title fight. His confidence in himself was so great he never thought about losing against two fine fighters as Larkin and Fontaine. A loss could have torpedoed his unification fight with Montgomery, so two months after the kayo of Larkin, Ike upended Monty.

In all three fights Williams was awesome. In the Juste Fontaine fight he neatly polished off a promising Milwaukee fighter in the fourth round of the non-title ten-rounder at the Philadelphia Arena. Juste held his own for three rounds. They stood toe to toe in the third. In the fourth a pile-driving right driven at short range caught him flush on the jaw. He got up at nine and tried to hold on. Williams, a great finisher, shoved Juste into a corner and showered him with blows from all directions. With the crowd in an uproar, referee Charley Doggert stepped in and ended the bout after 1 minute and 51 seconds of the fourth and final round. Fontaine, ranked number eight by *Ring* magazine, had rolled up an impressive string of knockout victories and shown an ability to come off the floor and go on to victory. But Fontaine couldn't make any comeback with Williams, who was like a tiger leaping at his prey as he rushed in for the kill with Fontaine helpless on the ropes. Ike was at his murderous best.

Fontaine's manager and trainer, the former welterweight champion Fritzi Zivic, remarked, "Ike was just too much for us," or anyone else near his weight for that matter. It was these 1947 knockout wins over

Juste Fontaine, Tippy Larkin, and Bob Montgomery that propelled Williams into his greatest year, 1948, in which he was declared "fighter of the year." Ike went on a tear, defeating welterweights Tony Pellone, Livio Minelli, and Kid Gavilan, giving the Kid five pounds and winning a unanimous decision. It was a rip-roaring fight at MSG. Gavilan had a 41–3–3 record and for the first time in his career kissed the canvas in the eighth round. The fight was very close, so they would meet again. But first Ike had to defend his lightweight championship. In *four months* Ike turned back the challenges of Enrique Bolanos, winning 15 rounds; Beau Jack, KO 6; and Jesse Flores, KO 10. With that business taken care of, Ike figured it was time for the return against Kid Gavilan. Back to MSG and again giving the Kid five pounds, on January 28, 1949, another war, with scores of 5–4–1, 5–4–1 and 4–4–2. Very close, with the majority decision going to Kid Gavilan. A ring classic.

Two months later they would meet again in the "rubber" match again at MSG. The gross was $96,000, huge for the times. It was an all-out battle again. This time Ike gave Gavilan a *nine-pound* advantage, the result being that Gavilan was just too strong and won unanimously. Gavilan was at his peak and heading for the welterweight championship. This trilogy could stack up with the Gatti-Ward fights of recent vintage. That's the barn-burners, they were.

Ike would defend his title two more times, against the very tough Bolanos for the third time and Freddy Dawson, kayoing Bolanos and winning a close unanimous decision over Dawson. Williams was having pure hell making the 135-pound weight; he was very weak for both Bolanos and Dawson. Ike would not defend his title again until May 25, 1951, 18 months after the Dawson defense. The boxing brass was putting the heat on Ike to defend or they would strip him of his title. Ike held out as long as he could, but he finally agreed to go through the torture of making 135 pounds for the challenger Jimmy Carter. The weight making almost got Ike killed. He took a frightful beating, down a number of times, and finally being stopped in the 14th round, losing his precious championship. Carter weighed 133, Ike a very weak 135. Williams should have retired and called it a career after this fight, but he didn't. He would go on to fight 16 more times in the next four years, losing seven times.

By the time Ike met Chuck Davey, he was only going through the motions. The promoters and the TV people were grooming Davey. He was the TV darling, and he needed *name* opponents he could beat to pad his record. Ike was a shell of his former self. He would make excellent cannon fodder for Davey. A win over Ike Williams would look good on his undefeated resume. Ike would be stopped in the fifth round. He caught everything Davey threw. The referee stopped the bout with Williams still on his feet. Both weighed 145 pounds. Ironically Rocky Graziano, another former champ engaging in his last fight, would be thrown to Davey like a piece of raw meat, which would help Davey get his title shot at Kid Gavilan. Gavilan slaughtered Davey; he simply was not in the Kid's class. The TV darling drifted off into oblivion as far as his career in boxing went.

In his last two fights, he fought his old rival and former lightweight champ Beau Jack. The two former champs figured their names could still bring in some pesos even if their best fighting days were long gone. They fought both fights in Jack's hometown of Augusta, Georgia, and struggled to a ten-round draw in the first fight. In the second fight Ike stopped Beau Jack. Beau was unable to come out for round nine. Ike weighed about nine pounds more than Beau. Both made their last paychecks that night of August 12, 1955. Both ended their careers and never fought again. Ike and Beau, along with Bobcat Bob Montgomery, were the cream of the lightweights for nearly a decade, Ike being the best of the three greats. Ike fought the Bobcat two times, losing the first by knockout and evening up the score by kayoing Bob the second time around. They never fought the "rubber" match. Williams fought Beau Jack four times, winning by kayo twice, decision once and a draw. The three of them were real blasters, never in a dull fight.

Along "Jacob's Beach," it was known that Ike's manager was Connie McCarthy, but behind the scenes was the man who pulled the strings, that being Blinky Palermo, an all-around "bad egg" according to the police. He was called many names, like racketeer and no-goodnick. But Blinky could move a fighter and get his fighters good money matches, which he did for Ike, including the shot at the title. But the *money*, oh the money. Poor Ike never got the full bread he earned. Blinky would get the lion's share of the loaf, much like Don King's share of his fighters' purses today. I lost count of the fighters taking King into court trying to get their rightful share of the money.

That was why, and Ike testified before a Senate hearing to the fact that after he retired he wasn't as well off as he should have been. He lived out his life on very modest means. How hard that man fought, and he claimed some fights he wouldn't even get paid. Other hands gobbled up the money. One's heart goes out to Ike; he never got his just rewards.

There is one thing they could not steal from Ike: The *glory* of being one of the greatest lightweights that ever lived. Ike went to the Boxing Hall of Fame in the sky on September 5, 1994, at age 71. His career span was from March 1940 to August 1955, 15 years and 5 months. He fought a total of 154 fights, won 125, lost 24, and drew 5 times. He scored 60 knockouts. He fought the best men in two divisions. In his prime he was unbeatable.

Ike's Outstanding Kayo Wins

1. Tippy Larkin
2. Bobby Ruffin
3. Bob Montgomery
4. Enrique Bolanos
5. Johnny Bratton
6. Beau Jack
7. Cleo Shans
8. Freddy Dawson
9. Vic Cardell
10. Juan Zurita
11. Eddie Giosa
12. Gene Burton

His Outstanding Decision Wins

1. Kid Gavilan
2. Joe Miceli
3. Lester Felton
4. Willie Joyce
5. Lulu Constantino
6. Sammy Angott
7. Luther "Slugger" White
8. Tony Pellone

The Garfield Gunner

Tippy Larkin—the name sounds like that of a movie star or super-hero. He was handsome enough to be an actor, but he wasn't. Superhero? Might have been, but his chin wouldn't let him. What he was was a brilliant boxer-puncher in the lightweight and welterweight ranks for over a decade.

In the 1930s and '40s, the sport of boxing had many Italian-American fighters. Some of them took Irish names for the simple reason that being Irish could help sell tickets and also help get the decent matches needed to move a boxer along. Our hero's real name, Antonio Pilleteri, chose the name of Tippy Larkin and would make it and Garfield, New Jersey, famous. Born there November 11, 1917, he would become one of New Jersey's most well-known boxers.

The year was 1935 when Tippy, armed with his Irish name but also with those "fine Italian hands," turned pro. His professional bow was a four-round decision loss. He then ran off twenty straight wins—fourteen by kayo. Boxing people took note quickly. Tippy showed he was a fine boxer; all he needed was more experience against the fighters of the day, and the next few years would supply it.

Johnny Schibelli would win a six-round decision over Larkin to stop his streak at twenty, but Tippy had already KO-ed Johnny earlier. Chang Collura would defeat Tippy next. Larkin would get hunks a few months later, beating Collura two times in six-rounders, all in Newark, New Jersey. The next fighter to give Larkin trouble was Mickey Duca. Larkin fought Duca, a rugged fighter, three times, losing the first two eight-rounders before gaining the win in their third eight. All three fights were fought in Newark. Every great fighter seems to have difficulties with a certain opponent. In Larkin's case it would have to be Mickey Duca. They never fought again, so Duca had the edge, winner two out of three. Tippy was learning fast and becoming an artful dodger who could slip and slide and parry blows like none before or after. He was becoming a pro's pro. He could feint an opponent out of position and make him look like a clumsy novice with his on-target counterpunches. But Larkin had a problem, a handicap, and it would come out later.

Tippy also had a Jersey rival that he had to take care of. And that he did. The rival was Freddie "Red" Cochrane. They first clashed in Newark in an odd-scheduled nine-rounder won by Tippy. He would fight Cochrane four more times in the next 17 months and win a decision each time, the last fight being a 15-rounder. It must have been clear at the time that Larkin was Cochrane's master. Talk about having someone's number. Amazingly, Cochrane would go on to upset Fritzi Zivic and win the Welterweight Championship of the World. None could blame the Elizabeth, New Jersey, redhead for never fighting Tippy again. Cochrane had to believe *five* times on the short end is enough. All their fights were crowd-pleasers.

Larkin's next decision loss would be in his hometown to the fine English fighter Jackie "Kid" Berg. The amazing thing about it is Larkin would fight another 13 years and 85 more fights and never lose another decision. He had the experience now and could not be beaten on points; that's the great boxer he was.

The first fighter to put the long snore on Larkin was crazy, left-hooking, Brownsville Bum, Al "Bummy" Davis. Bummy was a rough, tough street-type fighter whose main weapon was a devastating left hook. Opponents would beware when Bummy would spread his legs out wide and dig his left foot into the canvas. A Howitzer left hook would follow. He caught Tippy in the fifth round of their Madison Square Garden bout with that famous hook, and that was it for Larkin—Tippy's first knockout defeat. When Bummy landed that hook squarely, anybody would go. Proof of it was the night he kayoed the lightweight champion of the world Bob Montgomery with that one punch in the first round for a huge upset. Lucky for Montgomery it was a non-title fight.

Tippy's problem surfaced. His jaw failed him, and it would again in his very next fight. Less than three months after the Bummy Davis fight, Larkin was back in the Garden against power-punching Lew Jenkins. Talk about nerve on Larkin's part. Tippy was flattened in one round. Terrific knockout punchers could kayo Larkin, and he would be kayoed ten times in his career. But Tippy avoided no one. He took on such bangers as Henry Armstrong, Beau Jack, Ike Williams, Lew Jenkins, Al "Bummy" Davis and the heavy-punching Irvington, New Jersey, Milkman, Charley Fusari, twice. Armstrong, Beau Jack, Williams and Jenkins were all champions, quite a murderers' row. There was no doubt about it, Larkin had a problem, a major handicap especially for a fighter, a fragile chin, better known to boxing people as a glass jaw or a China chin.

Of course Tippy knew this the first time he ever laced on a pair of gloves. Some fighters are gifted with the ability to absorb heavy punches to the head and fight on. Not Larkin. A large majority of boxers quit and give up on the idea of becoming a pro fighter after a few sparring sessions in the gym where they are tagged a few good ones. Not Larkin. Know full well no matter how great a boxer you can become, you are going to get nailed from time to time. If you can't take a good punch, you would be better off to give up the idea and get out while you are still in good health. Not Larkin.

Tippy loved boxing and always dreamed of becoming a success at it. He believed the only way to be that success was to become a slick elusive master boxer who could avoid the big bombs. He put his whole heart and soul into becoming a fighter who could go against the best and win. He was fully aware that every fight he would have, and he had 154, he would have to be able to dodge those bombs. His jaw was fragile enough that every opponent he faced was a threat; only ten got through in his 17-year career. The wonderful thing about it was Larkin realized his dream; he was a huge success as a fighter, and he did win the Junior Welterweight Championship of the World.

On his way to that title, Larkin, besides the soft chin, had another problem: he would be fighting in an area that manufactures the best fighters in the world. He'd be going up against the best in the New York–New Jersey area. It had the best trainers, gyms, and talent the world over. The fighters struggled to make names for themselves in the huge club fight circuit that was Newark, Trenton, Elizabeth, Camden, Jersey City, Atlantic City, etc. They had shows going six nights a week. New York had multiple shows going Monday through Saturday. Fights were available; a fighter could fight often and learn his trade like nowhere else. Some of the fighters of the time fought three times a week in the prelims in these clubs. Main-event fighters often fought three times a month. The great Beau Jack, promoter Uncle Mike Jacobs' million-dollar baby, fought many main bouts in the Garden. In 1944 he fought *three* main bouts in one month there. A record. There were hundreds of fighters in the area, and damn good ones. Tippy would become part of it, glass jaw and all.

What a grand and glorious time for fight fans. Jersey boasted five world champions in the late forties. Cochrane at welterweight, Larkin at junior welterweight, Ike Williams lightweight, Gus Lesnevich at light heavyweight and ole Jersey Joe Walcott at heavyweight champion. And get this, they were undisputed, non-alphabet, real champions. Amazing.

Back to the drawing board for Larkin; after the two-kayo losses back to back, things weren't exactly rosy. Tippy's career could be at an end. Being the warrior he was, Larkin went on a winning streak of 23 in a row, with five wins over the likes of Maxie Fisher, Carmine Fatta, Chester Rico, and Lee Rodak, and two wins over Freddie Archer, a kayo and a decision over his Jersey rival. The second Archer win set up the title match for the vacant New York world lightweight title against the popular Garden favorite Beau Jack. They met on December 18, 1942, at the Garden, and Jack was able to land his bomb and flattened Larkin in the third round. One sportswriter quipped, "Larkin seems to have a fascination of the Madison Square Garden ceiling." His poor attempt at humor stunk. Larkin fought bravely in all his fights. Brave is hardly the word for it. In his very next fight after the Jack kayo, Larkin would take on the great Hammering Henry Armstrong, the only man to hold three titles at once, featherweight, lightweight, and welterweight, and he even fought the middleweight champ to a draw. Homicide Hank kayoed Tippy in the second round at San Francisco in March of 1943. Amazingly this was Larkin's first fight being fought on the West Coast. Tippy was truly a metropolitan-area fighter, thus his immense popularity in that region.

After Armstrong, Tippy would reel off 28 straight with only one no contest sprinkled in. He would go undefeated in 1944, 1945 and 1946. Nineteen forty-four was a very good year for Larkin. Four bouts at Madison Square Garden, two kayo wins, a decision and a draw. The first was a rousing draw with the very talented and tough Bobby Ruffin. Next, a

34

ten-round decision over top-ranked Lulu Constantino. Then a third-round kayo win over fellow Jerseyan and superb boxer Allie Stolz, and finishing with an emphatic kayo over his Jersey rival Freddy Archer. This was Freddy's third loss to Larkin, second by kayo. Archer was rushed to the hospital with a bad concussion after this bout. These four fights earned Larkin two more Garden events for 1945—good wins over Willie Joyce and tough Nick Moran. In 1946 Larkin was back at MSG whipping Nick Moran again in another pleasing fight. This set up a title shot for Tippy. He would face Willie Joyce for the vacant Junior Welterweight Championship of the World. The fight would take place in Boston on April 29, 1946. This title had lain dormant for years, but it would now be revived. This would be the second fight between the two; Larkin had won the earlier bout.

Boston fans were treated to one of the greatest fights seen there in years. Tippy came in at 139½ pounds to Joyce's 138¼ pounds. A fast finish by Larkin won him the fight and the Junior Welterweight Championship of the World. Larkin was dropped three times in the third round for counts of eight. Tippy called on all his courage and ability to finish the round. If the fight was held in more recent years when the foolish three-knockdown rule was in effect, Larkin would have lost by kayo and his dream of becoming a champion would have been dashed. In 1946 that stupid rule was unheard of. Larkin came back in the fourth, and it was a donnybrook all the way and anyone's fight going into the 11th round of a 12-rounder.

Boxing writers wrote that the fight was an awesome match up. The pugilistic workmanship was a work of art. Tippy was at the top of his game demonstrating his craft to perfection. This match left the spectator and the officials in awe. Such artistry is rare today. Larkin won the 11th and 12th and the fight with stinging left jabs and straight right crosses. This fight was so good there had to be a rematch. Joyce, a great little battler of the Henry Armstrong mold, deserved a return bout.

Back to that three-knockdown rule, I've seen many fighters floored two times and then "pushed" down for the third "knockdown," giving their opponent a knockout win. Two cases are recalled off the top of one's head where this rule would have changed boxing history. Marcel Cerdan would have never become middleweight champion had the rule been in effect in his bout with Anton Raadik, the tough Estonian. In the final, tenth round, Raadik would blast Cerdan to the canvas three times. Cerdan barely rose to make the final bell and win the decision he rightly deserved. If the rule was in effect, Cerdan would have become a kayo victim in round ten and lost the opportunity to go on to the middleweight championship. Archie Moore would have lost his title to Yvon Durelle, the Canuck flooring Moore three times in the first round. The silly rule would have given Durelle the title by first-round kayo. Instead, Moore came back to flatten Durelle in the 11th round, as did Tippy from the three knockdowns to become champion. Four months later, Larkin would defend his title in the return with Willie Joyce at Madison Square Garden in another great fight with a decision win, his third over Joyce.

In February of 1947, Larkin was back in the Garden against the new undefeated rage, the power-punching Irvington, New Jersey, Milkman, the blond bomber Charley Fusari. Charley threw his usual "million" right-hand bombs. He scored a ninth-round knockout, having Larkin down a total of five times, two knockdowns ending it in the fatal ninth.

Just five weeks later Larkin would meet Billy Graham, New York City's superb boxer, in the Garden ring. When that fight was announced I recall having a brainstorm to go big time. Myself and a school buddy who attended fights with me at Elizabeth, New Jersey's, Twin City Bowl and the Armory decided to go to the top: New York City's Madison Square Garden. It would be a lifetime dream come true, all fourteen years of it. We would save our money and go to see Larkin vs. Graham. We worked hard setting pins and collecting and selling scrap iron to make enough money for the train fare and the tickets for the fight.

I'd get to see my favorite fighter fight a terrific boxer like himself; it should turn out to be a classic. I'd also see the Garden for the first time. I couldn't wait for the days to pass for this great event.

Tippy didn't disappoint. I saw the greatest boxing match of my life. No match has topped it since. It reminded me of a fencing duel, much like Errol Flynn dueling with Basil Rathbone in the movies *Captain Blood* and *Robin Hood*. Smart boxing always reminded me of fencing or ballet. Hell, that's how a 14-year-old thinks. Truly, though, it was a boxing purist's masterpiece. Both boxed beautifully. The only fight I can recall that came close to that kind of brilliant boxing was Willie Pep's second fight with Sandy Saddler, a fight in which Pep had to overcome the brute strength of Saddler with a spectacular exhibition of pure boxing to take the fifteen-round decision and regain his title.

Billy Graham, a master boxer, had to be outmastered, Larkin made it a clinic. He used the first round as a feeling-out process, then romped to the decision victory, taking nine rounds on one judge's card. *Ring* magazine, the bible of boxing, had this comment, "Larkin won hands down and gave Garden fans a display of craftsmanship they will never forget." How very true. The *Ring*'s great artist and writer Ted Carroll added, "Tippy was a defensive genius."

Larkin weighed 139, Graham 139¾. It was only Graham's third loss in seventy fights. If Larkin had Graham's chin, he would have become a boxing immortal—the white Sugar Ray Robinson. Graham, who fought them all, was the possessor of an iron jaw. He was never stopped in over 100 ring battles. He later fought Kid Gavilan for the title and lost in a very disputed decision; he was then known as the "uncrowned welter-weight champion of the world."

We almost missed it all. When we got to the ticket booth, the man frowned and said, "You kids can't come in. You're not 16 and you must have an adult with you," claiming a New York state law. My heart sank. After all the work earning the money to get there and the wait, to be sent back on the train would be unbearable. We begged and pleaded as only kids can and finally won the guy over. He begrudgingly gave us the tickets and we were told to "lay low," meaning go in, be quiet, and don't make yourselves conspicuous by drawing attention to yourselves. That we did, but we even tipped the usher who seated us. Truly a highlight of a young boy's life. I figured the state law shouldn't apply to us; we were from New Jersey to root for the "Garfield Gunner."

Graham was gunned, but I do believe he learned a huge lesson from this fight. His career would only go up afterward.

Only three months later Larkin would take on, as usual, the best. Murderous punching Ike Williams, Trenton, New Jersey's, lightweight champion of the world. It was as if Tippy was putting himself in harms way to see if he really could get away from all the big punchers' bombs. Larkin would be again in the position to gaze at the Garden's ceiling as a fourth-round kayo victim. Eight wins later Larkin would be back in the Garden halting Willie Beltram, an upstart club fighter who was handled with ridiculous ease and kayoed in five rounds.

Tippy came to my hometown, Elizabeth, New Jersey, in 1948; he would meet the tough Jewish American 22-year-old Ruby Kessler. He and his brother Milton were from Coney Island, New York, and were raising hell in the fight clubs in New York City. Tippy would have his work cut out for him. The fight would be held at Twin City Bowl, August 31, 1948. This would be a return engagement; the men met at Eastern Parkway Arena, Brooklyn, three months earlier, with Larkin winning the decision in ten hard rounds. Kessler had come on strong in the last two rounds when Larkin seemed to weaken. Larkin's manager, the wily Angelo Pucci, agreed to the much demanded rematch, but being as crafty as he was, Angelo gave the nod only to an eight-rounder. Thus he took out an insurance policy for Tippy. I call that crafty managing.

Kessler in two recent Twin City appearances impressed local fans by giving the streaking Charley Fusari a rousing fight in front of a packed house, which set a money record for Elizabeth. Ruby came back after the tough Fusari fight to kayo the rugged Ross Anzalone in the last round of a thriller. This made Larkin vs. Kessler huge, so 1,700 fans turned up and were treated to a boxing clinic headed by the old teacher, Tippy Larkin. After all, he didn't need that insurance policy obtained by Pucci.

Larkin was at his best that night. It was fantastic. One had to feel sorry for Kessler; the ever-trying, hard-hitting lad was too busy trying to avoid Larkin's snakelike left jabs and jarring right hands to ever unload his big guns. He seldom tagged Tippy in the entire fight, a complete rout for Larkin, and it was well worth the price of admission to watch this great boxer. I enjoyed it immensely. The two wins over Kessler earned Larkin a rematch with the hard-punching Charley Fusari. They would meet in Jersey City. Fusari would win by kayo again. Unlike their first fight where Tippy was down many times, he would not be floored this time. Although taking a severe pummeling, he refused to go down, the referee stopping it in the sixth round. Larkin should have retired and called it a career after this fight, but fighters being just that, he refused to admit to himself he was through. He plugged on. This meant 14 more fights and allowing three more kayo losses tacked onto his record by fighters who couldn't punch their way out of a large wet noodle. It would give Tippy 11 more wins, nine by decision (he couldn't lose on points) and two kayo wins.

So basically Larkin's whole career was built around whether his jaw could hold up against the best punchers in the world and whether with this glaring disability he could win a world title. Yes, he did. A world champion he was, and a moneymaking pro with a satisfying career. He had accomplished his goal.

Trainers, in an attempt to strengthen their fighters' ability to absorb a good punch, stand behind their fighters with a towel around their jaw, holding both ends of the towel behind the head, one end in each hand held tightly. The fighter is then told to push forward and down on the towel, which produces a large strain on the neck muscles. This exercise is then included in all future workouts. Does it help? Only the fighter can say. If in upcoming fights he starts to take punches better than before, you could credit the towel method. Other trainers use a ten-pound weight attached to a skullcap head harness; the fighter sitting in a chair would then lower his head until the weight hit the deck, then pull up on the weight to the proper sitting position. This put all the pressure on the neck muscles. More weight could be added, and of course more repetitions if the method was proving successful to the fighter's ability to "take it." Of course some trainers claimed neck muscles had nothing to do with a fragile jaw. They believe you have to be born with the ability to take a punch. After all, how many fighters in all boxing history completed a full career without ever being knocked out? Think about it. The fact is, you probably would be pressed to find a dozen. Start with Marciano and Tunney.

That takes care of the jaw; how about terrific punchers? Many fight buffs believe you cannot be taught how to develop a huge punch. Punchers are born with that power. It is believed Tippy Larkin tried many methods to strengthen his jaw, but I believe he failed simply because it can't be done. One has to play the cards they are dealt in life. Tippy had a bad card there, and it probably was the joker. But I believe Tippy kicked that joker's ass, and he did it his way.

After that second Fusari fight, as we mentioned earlier, Larkin went on to the bitter end. He would win six in a row against jaded opposition and earn a fight in New Orleans with the highly touted Bernard Docusen. Again, he took a beating; Tippy couldn't answer the sixth-round bell. He was buried in an avalanche of punches from the light-hitting Filipino. Both of Larkin's eyes swollen shut, Angelo Pucci called a halt.

Still Larkin wanted to fight on; he won three more fights, then met a young kid out of the prelims by the name of Joey Lupo in Newark. The bout was stopped at the start of the second round. Larkin had developed a sprained ankle. Even his body was telling him to quit, but Tippy would win two more fights against a ham-and-egger, Maurice Jenkins. In Larkin's prime, Jenkins wouldn't be accepted as a sparring partner for him. Yet Jenkins lasted ten rounds with Tippy in both fights. That's how far Larkin had slipped.

Tippy was then matched with Steve Marcello, an up-and-coming kid. On December 29, 1952, the site, Providence, Rhode Island, Tippy was down twice and stopped in the fourth. This was Larkin's last fight. Larkin had an outstanding career, a superb boxer, and a good puncher, having scored 58 kayos in 150-odd fights.

Twenty-one years later I had the good fortune to meet up with Tippy in the lobby of Madison Square Garden; the date was December 14, 1973. He was wearing a navy blue topcoat and looked like he was still in fighting trim. He had a full head of hair and looked great. One couldn't believe that here was a man who fought all the best, for years in two weight divisions, barring nobody. He was still ruggedly handsome but he had that damn cigarette dangling from his lips. I always frowned on fighters that smoked, a reflex action on my part, but Tippy looked so good for an instant it seemed he was still campaigning. Hell, Larkin had retired two full decades past.

He was very cordial as we shook hands, and he autographed the book I bought from him. He, along with about a dozen other former fighters, were helping Willie Pep, the great former featherweight champion, sell his book, *Friday's Heroes*. They were all enclosed in a long wooded rectangular makeshift counter. Each fighter had a large card with his name on it set before him. A fan could walk up, buy the book and have it autographed by the fighters of his choice. On hand were, of course, Willie Pep, also Sandy Sadler, Larkin, Tami Mauriello, Steve Belloise, Freddie Russo, Chester Rico and Joe Miceli, plus more I can't remember. I prized that book but lost it forever when I loaned it to a former fighter and never got it back. Don't ever loan anything to a fighter;

they simply forget to return it. All they got on their mind is boxing; they eat, sleep and breathe boxing.

I'll never forget that night. I did get to meet Larkin, and then I went upstairs to see Jerry Quarry score a smashing one-round kayo over Earnie Shavers. A great boxing night indeed. An example, Earnie Shavers was one of the hardest punchers in heavyweight history. He, like Larkin, had that "handicap" of a fragile jaw. On account of that chin, Shavers never became a champion. He lost all the big ones. On the other hand, Larkin overcame the jaw problem by his ability to avoid most of the bombs. He had to avoid big punches in *all* of his 154 fights. Each *round* fought by Tippy was a crisis. That's how fragile his jaw was. In the hundreds of rounds fought in his lengthy career, seven bombs got through to kayo Tippy. That's a damn small percentage. This writer discounts three-knockouts that came at the end of Tippy's career when he should not have been fighting, one coming on a sprained ankle.

Terrific punchers, four of them world champions whose business was getting the kayo across, delivered all the seven kayos scored against Larkin. That's what made them great. Sometimes it seemed Tippy delighted in flirting with disastrous punchers, as if to prove to himself he could do it. Twice after suffering major kayo defeats, in his next fight, he'd be right back in there with another bomber.

Truly, no excuses for Larkin are intended here. He needs none. Larkin fought the best and dodged none. With his handicap, he still was able to become champion and build a fine record, with wins over the top contenders of his day. He was a champion of boxers, a delight to watch. He simply could not be outboxed. He could also punch hard enough to keep most opponents honest.

Boxing, especially New Jersey boxing, will never forget the "Garfield Gunner," Tippy Larkin. That was some ride, Tippy. Larkin passed away January 1, 1992, at age 74. Rest in peace. Give the angels up there in that big squared ring in the sky a treat and shadowbox a few rounds for them. It would be a thing of beauty they never seen before.

School of Local Ring Greats: New Jersey's Laurel Garden and Meadowbrook Bowl

The story you are about to read is fondly dedicated to the memory of the famous arenas that were once Laurel Garden and Meadowbrook Bowl, both located in Newark, New Jersey. Each was made of wood and concrete and was destroyed by time and the wrecking crews. But what could not be destroyed is the fistic history the old-time prizefighters, especially the Jersey boxers, made at those sites. They supplied a generation of fight fans' thrills and memories that will never be forgotten. From the wide-eyed preliminary fighter to the semifinalists to the main-event contenders and champions.

Hopefully, Laurel Garden and Meadowbrook Bowl, and the gladiators who fought there, will remain a superstructure in New Jersey boxing nostalgia. The beat goes on.

As we see it, the old-time boxers who were the gladiators and warriors of the prize ring of years past are being forgotten by the fight fans of today. It seems boxing writers do not hasten to write stories about those fine fighters, thereby plunging them deeper into obscurity. The loser is the fight fan. He or she may never read about the life and times of fistic greats such as Stanley Ketchel or Joe Choynski or even Billy Conn, just to name a few as examples. It is very sad. Therefore, I find it my obligation to write a story on the old-timers, champions all, whether they won a title or not, with the focus on New Jersey boxers.

To find a foundation or stage for the story, I selected Laurel Garden and its sister arena Meadowbrook Bowl, both located in the city of Newark, New Jersey. Laurel Garden wasn't air-conditioned. In the early days there was no such thing. Later on they did without. The promoters merely held their weekly fight cards at Laurel in the winter months and then went outdoors for their spring and summer shows at the Meadow-brook Bowl, an open-air arena.

As a young boy, the first time I made my way up the Laurel Garden steps to the cheap seats in the balcony I wondered, would these creaking stairs hold the heard of human flesh rushing up to the top in a mad rush to obtain a seat at the railing? It reminded me of the Armory in Elizabeth, which had the same setup. The musty smell of the stairway wasn't unpleasant; it was more like the smell of old wood, and it made me wonder some more, "how old is this place, and is it a fire hazard?" Yet it was a thrill for me to be at the Laurel, having heard of it all my life, a very famous boxing place. I knew the greatest fighters of the twentieth century fought in the Laurel ring, champions like Mickey Walker, James J. Braddock, Max Schmeling, Tony Canzaneri, Harry Greb, Billy Petrolle, etc., etc., with hundreds of others who plied their trade in this building. Laurel-Meadowbrook would be the beginning, the crossroads and the end of many fighters' careers. These two arenas were considered a finishing school for champions who graduated from them. Others fell by the wayside, still others into oblivion.

It all started in the 1920s. Laurel was operated as a beer hall. In the mid–1920s it became an arena for wrestling and boxing matches. The promoters had Monday boxing and Thursday wrestling. One could take a bus down to 457 Springfield Avenue, Newark, and arrive at Laurel, and for less than a dollar (in the '20s and '30s) see a great night of fisticuffs or wrestling. Promoter Willie Gilzenberg and Babe Culnan had Carmine Bolotti as their publicist and matchmaker, along with Duke Stephano. These were real McCoy boxing men who were giants for New Jersey boxing and the city of Newark. When they constructed a boxing card, it was almost certain they would use a national name in the main event pitted against a local or state talent. The prelim bouts would be made up of all local fighters such as city of Newark boys from different wards battling each other, or fighters from nearby towns like Elizabeth vs. Paterson. It made good rivalry, and each fighter had his following to fill the seats. The main-event big shot could be a boxer biding time while awaiting a title shot or a former champion still able to draw with his name and yet be a test for the local lad.

In the late '20s and early '30s Laurel was even used as a roller skating rink on nights other than the boxing and wrestling shows. Wrestling fell apart in the early '40s but boxing continued on until the building was finally demolished in the mid–1950s.

And what a role boxing played in that arena for over a quarter of a century. Punches were thrown by the best fighters in the world. The blood, sweat and tears, the dreams achieved and the dreams dashed. The champions and would-be champs all had their evening at Laurel-Meadowbrook. The fans, they had a ball. They benefited the most, getting top-talent shows for their dollar, and memories that would last a lifetime.

Let the reader now get a rundown on some of the great fights that were fought at these two fight arenas. The writer will cover fights I was familiar with and those that I attended, and we will wind up with the *greatest fight ever held* at Laurel Garden or Meadowbrook Bowl.

We all know about the previously mentioned greats that fought in the two rings. Tony Galento started his career at the two arenas. He fought many times there, winning and losing. Here are thumbnail sketches of some of the gladiators who graced the Laurel and Meadowbrook rings:

Tony Galento

Tony Galento started his career at Laurel. One of New Jersey's top heavyweights. In 1939 he came a whisker away from winning the heavyweight title in a thriller with Joe Louis. Joe had to come off the floor to stop the Orange, New Jersey, native. Galento had a lengthy career, beating some of the top men of the day. A fan favorite.

Abe Simon

Abe Simon was a huge Jewish-American heavy. He stood 6'4" tall and weighed between 250 and 260 pounds. At the time it was rare to see a heavyweight of that size ranked in the top ten. This New Yorker stopped off at Laurel in 1940 to face Jersey Joe Walcott, the usual ranked fighter against the local boy. Simon was on his way to two title shots at

Joe Louis. He knocked out Jersey Joe in six rounds. A year later Simon met Joe Louis for the first time and managed to last 13 rounds with the Brown Bomber. That was considered a feat in itself, so he would get a return bout with Louis. Joe always did better in return bouts, and he kayoed Simon in six rounds. What was ironic about the Simon-Walcott fight at Laurel was that both fighters would get *two* cracks at Joe Louis and his championship.

Jersey Joe Walcott

This Merchantville, New Jersey, boxer was an in-and-outer early in his career, mainly because the country at that time was struggling back after the Great Depression. Joe had a wife and six kids to support. He took any job he could get and used boxing as a supplemental income. He'd take fights when he could get them, most often as a last minute sub, in shape or not. I suspect Simon kayoed Walcott only because Walcott never trained for the fight. Joe and his family were on welfare, and if a fight was offered to Joe, he would jump at the chance.

After the Simon loss, Joe hardly fought at all for the next four years. He would make a comeback in 1944 by the urging of and backing of Felix Bocchicio, a local fight manager. With the proper training, diet, and Felix behind him, Walcott would rip right through the heavyweight division, scoring wins over Steve Dudas, Lee Q. Murray, Curtis Sheppard, Jimmy Bivins, Joey Maxim, Lee Oma, Tommy Gomez and Elmer Ray. Sheppard was called the "hatchetman," a terrific puncher, as was Tommy Gomez and Elmer "Violent" Ray. These wins made Walcott the number-one contender for Joe Louis's title. So seven years after his Laurel Garden loss to Simon, Walcott would get his shot at the title. And what a shot it was. A *huge* underdog, Walcott would drop Louis two times and lose a controversial decision. Ninety percent of the writers and fans thought Walcott had won easily, including the referee, Ruby Goldstein. Louis thought so too. He dejectedly left the ring before the decision was announced. He had to be called back to the ring to hear the verdict in his favor and the retainment of his precious title, over a thunderous chorus of boos. The public demanded a rematch. Again, Louis proved he was always better the second time around. He kayoed Walcott in eleven rounds again getting off the canvas to do so. Louis then retired after holding the title for *11 years and 8 months* and defending the crown *25 times*—two records that will never be broken.

Jersey Joe would not be denied. He would prevail. He set a record of his own by fighting three more times for the championship, a record setting *five* times. He gained the title on his fifth attempt. He was the oldest man to ever win that title, at age 37. George Foreman would shatter that feat years later. Walcott became New Jersey's second heavyweight champion, James J. Braddock being the first. Braddock, after winning the title from Max Baer, was dubbed the "Cinderella Man" for his accomplishment under almost impossible conditions. One could call Jersey Joe the same. They had a lot in common. Both men were Jerseyites. Both had come off the welfare rolls, both were family men and both had frequent losses in their early careers. Both were on comebacks when they won their title, and both were underdogs in their quest for the title.

Al "Bummy" Davis

Another Jewish-American fighter known as the "Brownsville Bum," the New Yorker had a left hook almost as potent as Tony Galento's nightstick hook. That is saying a lot because Bummy was only a welterweight. He came into the Laurel ring in 1940 to face Teddy Baldwin with 40 fights under his belt. He had only lost one, that to the great Lou Ambers. Davis had kayoed Tippy Larkin and the rebounding Tony Canzoneri in MSG bouts. At Laurel he stopped Baldwin in five. A few months later he would meet Fritzi Zivic at MSG in that infamous foul infested fight. Davis went berserk after being fouled by foul master Zivic and repeatedly kicked Zivic in the groin. He added to that by kicking the referee and the cops who entered the ring to restore order. A riot erupted around the ring. Davis was disqualified and suspended by the New York commission. The suspension would last only six months because a return bout was warranted after the notoriety the first fight had garnered. The return would be in a New York ballpark—the Polo Grounds. Zivic would kayo Davis in the much-hyped grudge match, stopping him in the tenth and final round. Davis was a real character, and he went on to score probably his greatest win with a one-round knockout of the current lightweight champ Bob Montgomery in a non-title fight. Bummy's left hook did it. The win earned him fights with Beau Jack and Henry Armstrong, which Bummy would lose at MSG. After his kayo loss to Armstrong, Davis put some wins together, which got him a match with the rampaging kayo artist and MSG golden boy Rocky Graziano. Davis was kayoed in the fourth round after his left hook had Graziano down in the second of a barn burner. Davis would fight one more time after the Graziano fight. Two months later Davis would challenge three gunmen who came to rob the bar his friend owned. Bummy coldcocked the first one and was reloading the left hook to take out the second. Both gunmen opened up on poor Bummy, and that left hook was silenced forever. That hook had accounted for 48 knockouts of his 60-odd wins, but it just didn't work against guns.

Many times in his career Davis was being outboxed and behind on points only to come up big with that huge left hook which he endlessly threw. This time it didn't save Bummy. Davis was 27 years old when he was gunned down.

Lem Franklin

When Lee Savold, a perennial heavyweight title contender, was kayoed by the great Joe Louis, he was asked by reporters, did anyone in his lengthy career hit harder than Joe? Without hesitation, Savold's answer was Lem Franklin. That is believable because Franklin had kayoed Savold, Jimmy Bivins, Curtis Sheppard, Tony Musto, and Abe Simon and was a top contender for Joe Louis's title. Only Joe's manager prevented that fight from materializing. His mentors figured no money could be made fighting a black contender, which Franklin was. Proof of the pudding is that Jersey Joe Walcott would get his shot in Louis's 24th defense only at a time when no white contender was available after Louis had kayoed Billy Conn and Tami Mauriello. Even then, the promoters figured they would call the number-one contenders fight with Louis a ten-round exhibition bout. The commission refused their request, and thus Walcott got his just dues. In Joe Louis's record you will notice in 25 defenses of the crown, only two black fighters got the shot—John Henry Lewis and Jersey Joe Walcott. John Henry, a former light heavyweight champ, got his bout with Joe only because he was Joe's best friend who needed one last payday. Joe Louis took John Henry out in one round, making it quick and painless.

Not getting his dream fight with Joe Louis, Franklin kept fighting the best in the division. It caught up with Lem in of all places the Meadowbrook Bowl, on July 24, 1944. He took on a Jersey trail horse, Larry Lane, and was knocked out in the ninth round. Lem Franklin died ten days later. Franklin was always noted as one of the hardest-hitting heavies of his day.

Gus Lesnevich

This Cliffside Park, New Jersey, light heavy fought often at Laurel on his way up to the Light Heavyweight Championship of the World. He was a very popular champion, always in a good fight. He had a tendency to cut easily, much like Chuck Wepner the Bayonne Bleeder. Gus could have been called the "Cliffside Park Bleeder" before Chuck ever thought of boxing. The boxing writers did dub Gus "The Russian Lion" because of his courageous, never-say-die style of fighting. A real role model. During and after his career was over, Gus and his good friend James J. Braddock, the former heavyweight champion, gave much of their time and money to any charitable organization that asked them for their help in obtaining funds. They would make personal appearances, speak at different functions, and assist in any way they could to earn a buck for the needy. Gus and Jim never forgot the vets at the VA hospitals either, visiting them often to keep up their spirits. Both were two just as great guys as they were champions.

Fritzi Zivic

This Pittsburgh, Pennsylvania, welterweight became world champion by defeating the great Henry Armstrong. Fritzi looked like a fighter, with his flattened nose and battered features. He was a throwback to the Henry Greb era. He could box and punch and was a master at foul fighting. Andrew Golota the foul Pole is a choirboy compared to Zivic. Even

Two-Ton Tony Galento couldn't match Zivic's tactics. He would fight anybody. Promoter Mike Jacobs would call Fritzi and tell him he had a fight for him at MSG, and Zivic wouldn't even ask the opponent's name or weight; he only asked "when, where, and how much?" He kept in shape simply by fighting often, sometimes four times a month. He amassed over 233 fights in a 19-year career. Fritzi fought long after he should have packed it in. He made money fighting the local heroes in their hometowns all over the U.S. of A. The local promoters wanted very much the name of Fritzi Zivic in the win column of the home-town favorite. Zivic lost most of the time but gave a good account of himself even though old and shopworn. If the local kid won, he could claim he beat a former world champion plus gaining experience. Every now and then, Fritzi would beat one of the upstarts. Zivic had fought the best men of his day; he took on Jake LaMotta four times when others dodged the Raging Bull. He managed one victory and three very close decision losses to the Bull. Fritzi beat Henry Armstrong two out of three. Sugar Ray Robinson beat Zivic twice in tough fights. Zivic also fought the feared Charley Burley three times, beating Burley once. When he lost the welterweight crown, which he took from Armstrong, he lost it at Ruppert Stadium, Newark, New Jersey, in July of 1941 to Freddie "Red" Cochrane on a 15-round decision, a huge upset for the Eliza-beth, New Jersey, redhead. Zivic got hunks on Cochrane a year later at MSG, winning in ten rounds. It was a non-title bout, so no crown for Fritzi. After his retirement, Zivic promoted fights and later became a trainer.

Ken Overlin

A middleweight champion—a great one. He had lost his title at MSG to Billy Soose and four weeks later tagged Ezzard Charles with his first loss. Ezzard was 20–0 as a pro and never lost an amateur fight. Ken changed all that. Overlin was a smart boxer; not much of a puncher, but he was a ring general. He knew every trick of the trade—truly a forgotten champion. Ken fought all over the United States, Australia, and Europe, and yes, Laurel Garden, much of the time when in the U.S. Navy.

Lou Duva

A Jerseyite, the fabulous Lou fought his heart out at both Laurel and Meadowbrook. Duva boxed in the prelims at both rings and ended his boxing career in Florida. Lou decided he would rather train fighters to throw punches instead of taking punches himself, and boxing benefited by his decision. Duva became a top trainer and manager and later a world-renowned promoter—a credit to boxing.

Jimmy Bivins

Bivins was a Cleveland, Ohio, lightweight who fought many heavyweights and beat them. He never got a title shot although he beat Gus Lesnivich, Melio Bettina, Tami Mauriello, Archie Moore, Jimmy was an all-time great. As his lengthy career was coming to a close he fought at Laurel, losing a ten-rounder to Sid Peaks.

Lee Oma

A heavyweight, Lee Oma called Buffalo, New York, his home. "The Clown Prince of Sock" was one of the strangest and most unorthodox heavyweights who ever lived. He seldom trained and was a chronic playboy and womanizer. The women liked him too because he was very handsome and a carefree spender. It was said by his trainer that Lee tried never to fight in the center of the ring. He mostly fought off the ropes because he needed them for support or his legs would give out. He played the ropes like a violin. He had to, since he seldom did roadwork. Although knocked out *20 times*, he went on a huge winning streak and gained a shot at the heavyweight championship—almost unbelievable but true. Most boxing writers of the day thought the only way Oma would ever get to see a heavyweight title bout was by buying a ticket, yet here he was fighting in MSG for the biggest prize in all sports, taking on Ezzard Charles. Oma actually gave a good account of himself. He staggered Charles a few times and had him cut, and one judge had it even going into the tenth round. In a strange and bizarre ending to the

50

fight, Oma dropped his hands to his sides and just walked away from Charles who chased after him with a couple of halfhearted shots to Lee's back. The ref had no choice but to stop it. Lee just ran out of gas. His body and brain told him it was the tenth round and it was time to stop. Lee had never seen an 11th round and never would. Yet he actually trained *ten days* for his shot at the title, a record for Oma.

When he felt like fighting, he beat the best—good heavyweights like Lou Nova, Joe Baksi, Tami Mauriello, Lee Savold and Gus Lesnivich. In his early career he fought often at Laurel and Meadowbrook. The last fight he had at Laurel was a ten-round decision over Tiger Ted Lowry, whose claim to fame was going ten rounds *twice* with Rocky Marciano, losing the decisions.

Lee Savold

Lee Savold was a St. Paul, Minnesota, heavy who later made New Jersey his home. Lee had a fantastic left jab, and it accounted for many broken noses among the heavyweights. He fought all the top men, including Joe Louis and Rocky Marciano. At one time he was named heavyweight champion by the British after kayoing their champion Bruce Woodcock.

Pat Comiskey

Comiskey was a Paterson, New Jersey, Irish-American who stood 6'4" tall and weighed 220 pounds. Pat was Lee Savold's stablemate and was taught the jab to perfection by Lee. He also had a booming right cross. He skyrocketed to the top, winning 29 of 30 fights with 25 kayos and then rushed into a huge fight with Max Baer, the former heavyweight champion. The fight would be held at Roosevelt Stadium in Jersey City. Baer, still a terrific puncher, kayoed the *19-year-old* in one round. Jack Dempsey was the referee. The fight was supposed to be a win for Comiskey with Pat then challenging Joe Louis for the crown. Everyone was looking for a Louis-Comiskey fight—that's how sensational this kid looked on the way to Baer. Old Max burst the bubble. Comiskey would fight another 11 years, threatening but never getting that title shot. Pat fought at both Meadowbrook and Laurel Garden.

Joe Baksi

Joe Baksi was a Kulpmont, Pennsylvania, rough, tough coal miner, a Jim Jeffries look-alike who was as strong as Jeffries and could body punch as good as him. Baksi had an iron jaw. He fought the best of his day and was ranked number one for a long while. He was stopped once on a badly cut eye from Ezzard Charles. He was never floored in his entire career of over 60 fights. One of the strongest heavyweights ever. Baksi fought Jim Holden of Elizabeth in a very good brawl won by Baksi, a ten-round decision at Laurel.

Tami Mauriello

A Bronx, New York, heavyweight, Mauriello started as a pro at the tender age of 15 and burned out and retired at age 26, another case of starting too soon. He was terrific, yet never met total maturity. How good would he have been if he started at 18 and fought his early fights at full strength and endurance? We will never know; very sad.

Tami, at age 17, lost a split decision to future middle king Billy Soose and kayoed Steve Belloise in one round, an amazing feat for a kid his age. Belloise and Soose were great fighters. Seven months later he fought Gus Lesnivich for the undisputed Light Heavyweight Championship of the World. Gus, an experienced, fine champion at age 26 with 60 fights behind him, was held to a 15-round split decision by the teenager. Many thought Tami deserved the duke. No fault of Gus, but it was a man fighting a boy. Imagine what Tami could have been if he and his managers had seasoned him more. As it was, Tami was finished at 26 while Gus was champion and retained his title and was at top form at 26. Such is boxing.

Tami was growing into a heavyweight. After Lesnivich, he moved up to that division. He was a good one and banged his way to a title shot at Joe Louis at the tender age of 23. It was short and sweet. In a riot of a first round, Tami caught Louis with a smashing right hand, driving Louis clean across the ring into the ropes, which saved Joe from a knockdown. Louis came back at Tami with his own right hand and dropped the youngster. Tami was up at nine. Louis came in to flatten him. Instead, he was caught with another Mauriello right-hand bomb, and again it drove him into the ropes. Joe came back with a vengeance. He hit Tami so hard that the punch actually lifted Mauriello off the floor. The shot was caught in a famous photo of the fight. It was all over in 2:09 of the first round. Tami went downhill after that loss, but he would stop at Laurel two times in his last year for two decision wins.

Bernie Reynolds

A Fairfield, Connecticut, heavyweight, Bernie Reynolds was a protégé of Gus Lesnivich and also managed by Joe Vella. It was only proper to write about Bernie, who headed a lot of shows at the two arenas in the later '40s and early '50s, a good action fighter who just remained on the fringe of the top ten. Whenever he stepped up into that range by taking on Ezzard Charles, Rocky Marciano, Joe Baksi, Cesar Brion, or even Jackie Cranford, Bernie was flattened. Reynolds, a handsome young man, was also a playboy who frequented nightclubs. So the story goes, if you care to believe those grocery-store checkout scandal newspapers, one night Bernie met up with a bigger playboy than himself with whom he engaged in some fisticuffs. The result, Robert Mitchum, the actor, kayoed Bernie. Evidently, Mitchum should also have been rated in the top ten. But we give Bernie his just dues; he was a crowd-pleaser and supplied many thrills for Laurel and Meadowbrook fans.

Joe Curcio

Joe Curcio was a Newark, New Jersey, middleweight. Very popular, he was known as "Indian Joe" by his friends. Although of Italian heritage, with his hatchet nose, he looked like an American Indian. Curcio turned pro at 17 and retired at 25. In eight years he packed in 100 fights. A southpaw, Joey could punch pretty well and box. From 1942 to 1949 he haunted

Laurel and Meadowbrook. He fought there 34 recorded times, with at least 15 main events. They could have renamed the two arenas "Indian Joe's Place." He also had another favorite spot that was my hometown, Elizabeth, New Jersey; he appeared there 25 times. This writer saw Joe fight a number of times and will always remember his will to win and never-ending drive. When he lost, he lost only to the best. An MSG fight with the great Sugar Ray Robinson ended with Joe a kayo loser in two rounds. He also lost to Rocky Graziano twice and Kid Gavilan once. His best wins were over Artie Towne, Cecil Hudson, Aaron Perry, Fritzi Zivic and Freddy Archer. He fought his rival, Bayonne battler Tony Riccio, *six times*, winning four. A real Jersey fighter was Joe Curcio.

Tony Riccio

Riccio was a Bayonne, New Jersey, middleweight. A fan favorite, Tony was always in demand. A real buzz saw that threw punches in bunches. The promoters liked Tony; he always gave a terrific fight. The amazing thing about Riccio was that in a career that spanned over 100-odd fights, he scored but five knockouts. He managed to beat some of the top fighters of the day. His losses to Sugar Ray Robinson and Charley Fusari could be excused. Riccio was one tough guy. He appeared at Laurel often.

Mike DeCosmo–Laurie Buxton Fight

Writing a story about the two arenas would be incomplete without the mention of this fight held on May 18, 1948. It was the first outdoor card of the season at Meadowbrook Bowl, and it was darn right cold. The night before, the boxing card at Twin City Bowl in nearby Elizabeth was called off due to cold temperatures. Not taking heed, the Newark promoters went ahead with the DeCosmo-Buxton fight. The fans that braved the cold and did not leave, as most did, during the prelims were rewarded with a ring oddity seldom if ever seen before.

DeCosmo, a hard-hitting southpaw from Elizabeth, New Jersey, and Buxton, an Englishman campaigning in the states, had a nip-and-tuck close fight going into the tenth and final round. Whoever would win the final round would more than likely win the fight, so both men poured it on. As the final bell rang, Joe Walker the referee stepped in to break it up and was caught with a haymaker flush on the jaw. He was knocked cold. Evidently, Joe's jaw was not as sturdy as his world famous brother, who was the "Toy Bulldog" Mickey Walker.

Joe was revived by the commission doctor, and he, as referee, was the sole judge under New Jersey rules at that time. The spectators had to wait until Joe's head cleared so he could score the final round and render a decision. Joe scored the last round for the Englishman, thereby giving him the victory 5–4–1 in rounds. When asked by reporters who hit him, Walker claimed he did not know. I think, as well as most of the fans present, that Walker knew that the only kayo puncher in that ring was the wild-swinging DeCosmo. By giving Buxton the last round, Walker got even with his fellow hometowner. Why would a ref give such a tight round to a foreigner and not to his fellow Elizabethan? A rocket scientist is not needed to figure that one out. The decision was roundly booed. Sorry, Mr. Walker, the fans are entitled to their opinions, and your vengeance stood out like a sore thumb. An alert photographer caught the action, and the photo is one of boxing's best. Walker is seen unconscious on the canvas. DeCosmo is seen going to Joe's aid and bending over the still form, but it actually looks like he is counting the ref out. Buxton stands over both in a fighting pose.

Artie Towne

A New York City middleweight who won 90 of 108 fights, Towne retired in 1959 in disgust, when he knew he would never get a title shot and couldn't get any meaningful fights. He became a mailman to support his family. Towne would die in the streets, a victim of knife wounds caused by two lowlifes who were after the monthly welfare checks they knew mailmen were delivering that day. In the tradition of Al "Bummy" Davis, Towne, a warrior, decided to defend the U.S. Mail with his bare fists. Just as gallant as Davis, Artie fought until he dropped. A fine husband, father and family man, Artie, like most boxers, was too brave for his own good. He was one of boxing's best.

Towne was a real ring wizard, a mechanic, with a style much like Charley Burley, another feared fighter who was avoided. Their non-flamboyant styles shooed away the promoters. They would rather use a Ray Robinson, Rocky Graziano or a Beau Jack who would draw in the fans and thrill them and bring them back for the next show. Only England, a country whose boxing buffs always cared for smart, stand-up fancy boxing, appreciated Towne's fine boxing ability. Artie had five fights there and won them all against the best England could offer. He often fought in South American countries for a payday. Listed are his wins over men who were name fighters and were willing to get in the ring with Towne: Yvon Durelle, Joe Blackwood, Bert Lytell, Joe Curcio, Buddy Farrell, Phil Saxton and Lavern Roach.

Johnny "Red" DeFazio

A featherweight to welterweight from Bayonne, New Jersey, Johnny "Red" DeFazio was a baby-faced terror who threw punches constantly and fought at both arenas often. A teenage crowd-pleaser who started at 15 and ended at age 21. DeFazio had over 50 fights in six years. At age 17 he fought two former world champions. Phil Teranova, a former featherweight champ, was boxed to a draw. DeFazio was kayoed by former lightweight champion Lew Jenkins, the Sweetwater, Texas, bomber.

DeFazio worked his way up to MSG semifinal bouts and main events at St. Nick's, the Garden's farm club. His biggest "win" was a draw with top contender Del Flanagan. In his fight with old pro Lew Jenkins, DeFazio got cocky with the former champ who was content to give the kid a boxing lesson and cop the decision. DeFazio's actions irritated Lew, who promptly flattened the upstart in the eighth round.

Johnny Red got involved with the mob and disappeared from the face of the earth. Other arena alumni who died of lead poisoning were Terry Young, Frankie Palermo and Johnny DeGilio.

Archie Devino

A Newark, New Jersey, featherweight, this superb boxer-puncher fought many times at the two arenas, from preliminary bouts to main events with the top fighters of the time. Archie simply punched too hard for his own good. Broken and bruised hands dogged him throughout his career and brought it to a premature end. Many times he had to cancel top bouts with men like Freddie Russo and Eddie Compo and others because of bad hands. In a fight with Johnny "Red" DeFazio, Archie lost the decision in a bout he should have easily won. His hands were badly swollen and bruised, thus keeping Archie on the defensive and earning DeFazio the win. Archie is a Post 25 member and an enhancement to the sport of boxing.

Don McAteer

Don McAteer was a New Jersey light heavyweight. Another Post 25 member who fought often at both arenas, losing only one of nine recorded fights there. Don was a light heavy who insisted on battling heavyweight contenders, giving away many pounds. This writer had the privilege of seeing Don fight at the Teaneck, New Jersey, Armory. He would take on Frankie DePaula, a murderous punching light heavy, and it was a war. The fight ended in a draw. They were matched again in another all-out brawl, with DePaula copping the decision. The two fights had the fans in frenzy, both slam-bang affairs. McAteer had already fought Tom McNeeley and Mike DeJohn, two top-ten heavyweights, winning over McNeeley and losing to DeJohn. He met DePaula right after the DeJohn fight, and when he met a man his own size, he fought two of his best fights ever. Yet he returned to fighting the big guys and took on large Chuck Wepner in a losing effort. Don was at his best at 173 pounds. What would have happened if Don had stayed in the light heavy division? My humble opinion—only good results. I pegged McAteer and DePaula as young men to be reckoned with in any future plans in the light heavy division. Their two battles, which many believed could go either way, were world class.

The 175-pound class was lucrative for DePaula, yet McAteer, a boxer who could stay right with DePaula, left for the heavyweights. It had to be that McAteer could not make 175 pounds anymore, thus forcing him into "no man's land," a position where a fighter is too big for light heavy yet too small for the heavyweights. If you weighed 176 pounds, you were officially a heavyweight. Your opponent would weigh much, much more. There was no limit after 175 pounds. The problem was finally solved with the birth of the cruiserweight division.

Phil Saxton

An Elizabeth, New Jersey, light heavyweight, Phil never lost a fight in New Jersey as an amateur or pro. He engaged in the greatest fight ever seen in the Laurel Garden ring. New Jersey boxing writers at the time agreed the Phil Saxton vs. Billy Black fight was the most thrilling ever held in Newark.

The *Newark Star Ledger* had Tony Marenghi as its boxing writer. The *Newark Evening News* had Willie Ratner at the helm. Both men, highly respected and well known, praised the young battlers for their "above-and-beyond" efforts. Phil went on to become light heavyweight champion of New Jersey. He was a champion in every sense of the word, not worldly but locally.

Saxton and his trainer-manager Pete Nozza is a story that should be told. They were the role models of what a relationship between fighter and manager should and *must* be for success, and above all, the good of the sport. The time was the mid–1940s and Phil was just trying to grow up amid all the chaos, shortages and mental tensions thrown on the people by the Second World War. The world was in turmoil; the two big bombs had been dropped on Japanese cities. Phil was this writer's friend, and any friend of mine had to box. I had been bitten by the boxing bug early in life. Being the kids we were, the war came second only to boxing. That summer we boxed in my yard. In the winter, we would spar in the cellar. Our heavy bag was a potato sack filled with newspapers and rags. Phil was bigger than I and well muscled, very strong, but he had an easy-going personality. We boxed so much we knew each other's punches before they were launched. Plus Phil was too big and powerful for me to give him a good workout. I decided that Phil needed new sparring partners. I became the matchmaker. I shanghaied every big tough kid I could find in our neighborhood, and there were many. Phil disposed of them all. I noticed Phil would let up on his spar mates; he didn't want to hurt them too badly. Was this the sign of a reluctant warrior? The war was over now, and in my mind I knew Pete Nozza would be coming home. A family friend and amateur boxer who also boxed in the Navy, winning the South Pacific lightweight championship, I thought Pete would train Phil and teach him the fine art of pugilism. We both hoped he would. Pete came home and after a while started training Phil for the Golden Gloves. Phil was approaching 16 and could get his AAU card.

It was an unlikely union of a former amateur boxer, who was a Navy war veteran and aspiring physical education teacher of Italian-American heritage, with that of a 15-year-old black kid born to a struggling family. Little did I know that Pete and Phil would become friends for life. Pete not only became Phil's trainer-manager but also acted as his big brother, and the feeling of respect for each other was mutual. When Phil got hurt with a punch, you could see Pete in his corner cringe from the same punch.

Pete Nozza was an extremely dapper, handsome young man with a gift of gab and a personality no one could dislike. He took like a duck to water in his new venture into the training of boxers. His athletic abilities could not be questioned. Pete, being a top athlete in high school, although weighing in at 135 pounds, was dubbed "the Mighty Mite" by the *Elizabeth Daily Journal's* boxing writer, Chris Zuzi, referring to Pete's football prowess on the gridiron. Nozza played guard on the Thomas Jefferson High School team. He later played guard for Panzer College and semi-pro ball with the Elizabeth Belmonts. A 135-pound guard who played offense and defense, he had to be tough. Pete was aiming at being a teacher of physical education on completion of his studies at Panzer.

Pete's regimen for training fighters was absolutely unique. He'd spend hours with Saxton on the "pads" and then get in the ring and spar with heavy "Punchin' Phil" and tell his protégé to "cut loose and keep me honest." That took mucho large testicles to tell a puncher like Phil. After the strenuous workouts, it was good to hit the showers, get dressed, and hurry upstairs—the gym was in the basement. The spar mates followed Phil and Pete from the gym to the first floor. This was Kirk Center in Elizabeth. On the first floor was a room I'd call a day-care room provided for the kiddies of the neighborhood. Since we did our training in the evenings, the day-care room was locked. The important item in that room was the piano. Pete would get to that piano simply by obtaining the keys from the caretaker. He happened to be a friend of Pete's who was a former lightweight, a very good one by the way. Old-timers might remember Frankie Duane from the Peterstown section of Elizabeth, New Jersey—Tippy Larkin's stablemate. Frankie was an ace of a person and a fine boxer-puncher.

Once in the room, Pete would sit down at the piano and play any song we'd request, from "Chopsticks" to classic Mantovani themes. Pete was an accomplished pianist and could also make an accordion jump. The music really settled the fighters down and relaxed them after the workouts. After the music Pete would drive everyone home. On the way, boxing styles and techniques were discussed, along with fatherly advice for anyone who asked for it. We were all high school students, and Pete would stress the importance of graduation. He would remind us all as he dropped us off at our homes, "Don't forget to do your homework." This was a man who if he had so chosen could have been right up there with the Charley Goldman, Ray Arcell, and Eddie Futch super trainers of the sport. Pete was more: he was a friend, a big brother, a trainer and above all, a teacher of worldly things, with the stress on boxing.

Pete always emphasized the left jab, it being the shortest distance from your left glove to your opponent's jaw. He'd build all the fighters' "other" weapons around a great jab. When Saxton started as a 160-pound novice in the New Jersey Golden Gloves, he had a fine left jab and a heavy right cross, but the right didn't have the leverage and accuracy Pete desired. They would have to work on it. Phil took the 160-pound title with three decision wins and one kayo. They were now ready to enter the Union County Diamond Gloves. Phil won the open 160-pound class by decision. All this time they worked on Phil's right hand. In his next fight with the same opponent, he decisioned in the Diamond Gloves; it would be a disaster for Dom Zimbardo. Dom was knocked out cold by Saxton's right-hand bomb. Zimbardo was out for ten minutes. Everyone was relieved when Zimbardo finally got up. Phil was now a deadly puncher with his right hand and would prove it throughout his career. Zimbardo, a good fighter, went on to the pros and was a main-event fighter.

I wondered if this emphatic kayo of Zimbardo, flat on his back, motionless on the canvas for so long, helped or hurt Saxton mentally. Knowing Phil's feelings and reluctance to hurt anyone, could this be a plus or minus to his career? Only time would tell.

Saxton went on to Laurel Garden to win the 175-pound open title with two smashing kayo wins. He then followed up with two more knockouts at Trenton, New Jersey, for the state AAU Light Heavy Crown. In all, Phil entered *five* tournaments in New Jersey and came away with *five* championships—some record for the high-school youngster. Laurel-Meadowbrook became Phil's lucky rings. He would never lose at either location.

Saxton turned pro at 18 and won his first three bouts impressively. He was then matched with Randall "Skeets" Starkey an undefeated (14–0, ten kayos) fighter from Maryland. They would meet at Ridgewood Grove Arena in New York. Both boys went at it hammer and tong. Saxton broke his right hand in furious early exchanges. He tried to continue fighting with one hand. The young warrior found out he couldn't fight such a heavy puncher as Starkey was with one gun. He needed more than that to keep Starkey off. Phil lost by TKO in the third round.

On the sidelines until the hand healed, Phil came back with a vengeance. He'd win six straight, earning a main event at Laurel against undefeated Billy Black. These two young men would engage in the fiercest and most thrilling fight ever held at the arenas. Both heavy right-hand punchers, they clashed in ring center, and there was no quarter asked or given. They literally tried to pound each other into the canvas. Saxton smashed a right-hand bomb off Black's jaw, putting Black in deep trouble, and if he had pressed his advantage he would most likely have kayoed Black right then and there in the first round. I believe the fear of hurting someone reared its head again, and reluctant Phil failed to finish Black before the bell. This would come back to haunt him because he would have the fight of his life on his hands. In the second and third rounds, Black was actually still trying to recover from that first-round blast, although battling all out. In the fourth it was Black's turn; he delivered a blistering body attack and then shifted to the head, dropping Phil. Saxton continued to take a pounding in the fifth and sixth rounds, getting floored in each session. He had been down a total of three times by now, and there was fear the referee might stop it. Each time Phil arose from the knockdowns, he kept punching back. In the seventh, Saxton started getting solid rights into Black's head. Then in the final round, the eighth, Saxton to win would have to kayo Black—and that is exactly what happened. He nailed Black with a terrific shot to the head, a vicious uppercut, staggering Black. Phil rained punches on Black until he finally crossed a booming right hand that put Black flat on his face. The dead game Philadelphian barely rose at nine, and as the referee, Joe Kukal, was wiping his gloves, Black stumbled backward and fell under the ropes, out cold. The fight was so furious fans were standing on their chairs cheering their heads off. Many boxing writers agreed it was the best fight held in Newark since the fight between heavyweights Al Walker and Big Bill Hartwell 20 years before. That fight was held at Newark Armory. Most managers and cornermen claimed Black-Saxton was the best ever in Newark's fistic history *period*. But positively it was the best scrap ever fought at Laurel-Meadowbrook.

Saxton and Black would meet again, and it was a carbon copy of the first fight. Saxton would be floored twice, but this time he'd win the eight-round decision in another donnybrook. Black never regained the form he displayed in these two fights and faded from the scene.

Seven months later Saxton would retain the New Jersey State Light Heavy Championship by defeating Jimmy Cerello, a good fighter from Hoboken, following with a win over Roosevelt LaBoard. The two wins earned Phil a semifinal eight-rounder at St. Nicholas Arena in New York City. His foe would be another Philly fighter, undefeated Richie James, a fine prospect who was making waves. Saxton, who it seemed was hell on Philly fighters, dropped James four times and ran away with the decision. Most felt after the fourth knockdown that Phil should have closed the show. Reluctant? Only Phil could say. This fight with his easy win over James was to have gotten Phil a main event in MSG, but Uncle Sam had other plans for the young boxer.

The Korean War was on, and Phil was drafted. He would serve two years overseas. I believe the time spent in the Army changed the course of Phil's boxing destiny. It derailed him, knocked him off track, simply because Phil did not continue to box as other fighters did while in service. Saxton did not lace on a glove for two years. He wouldn't box for anyone but Pete Nozza. This in no way helped Phil. He wasn't even around boxing people who would have kept the flame alive within his heart.

His first fight back, Joe Shaw, a tough journeyman, held a very rusty Saxton to a draw. Phil then scored a sensational first-round knockout at MSG, and the win got him a main event at Sunnyside Garden on Long

Island. His opponent would be the much-feared Artie Towne, a ranked light heavy who had trouble getting fights. Contenders cared little to tangle with Artie. Pete Nozza, Saxton's brain trust, figured it this way: first, he had all the confidence in the world in Phil, and Phil looked like he had regained his former skills from before his Army stint. He looked terrific in his last fight, and he could be up for the upset win.

On the other side of the coin, Towne recently had been looking a little ring worn. It might be time for a strong young puncher like Saxton to defeat Towne. A win over Artie would skyrocket Saxton's career and keep him sharply focused on boxing.

It looked like the strategy just might work because a week before Saxton was to meet Towne, Artie lost a ten-round decision in Detroit. It sure felt like upset was in the air.

The young pro was pitted against the old pro Towne with a great 86–13–1 win-loss record. It made Saxton the big underdog. So on that pleasant May night, Saxton entered the ring to take on his most formidable opponent in his young career. If you like smart boxing along with potent punching—Towne could also punch, having scored 40 kayos—then this fight was your cup of tea. Saxton would lose the unanimous decision, but the young man could take pride in his fantastic performance. He gave Towne all he could handle and boxed like a clone of Towne himself. The fight was fought at a fast, hard-punching pace, with Towne calling on all his experience to just win by a shade in each round. It was a classic. So much so that *Boxing Illustrated* rated Saxton in their top ten for Archie Moore's title. Other rating organizations followed suit. It was very rare indeed that an unranked fighter would become rated for a losing effort. It speaks volumes for Saxton's showing. Nozza's strategy almost pulled it off. The loss was really a gain for Saxton. Unhurt, he garnered a world of experience from the fight.

I recall after the decision was announced Towne came down the stairs of the ring, and I like a fool ran up to him and mocking him called out, "What's the matter, Artie? How come you couldn't flatten this kid?" Gentleman that he was, Artie grinned, shrugged his shoulders and said two words to me: "Kid's good." A fine compliment from a great fighter. He calmly walked on to his dressing room. I ordinarily refrain from such actions, but I was deeply hurt seeing my friend lose such a splendidly fought fight. Towne won, I agree, but Saxton also came away a victor.

The loss, however, did not sit well with Phil, even if it was only his second. He certainly had nothing to be ashamed of. Saxton completely lost his desire to fight. He lost two more fights and retired. Phil was just too gentle a man. He did not have the so-called killer instinct fighters are supposed to have. Although you couldn't say that after the Black brawls. I believe that was a "will to win" trait.

It was a sad day for boxing when Pete Nozza called it a day after the retirement of Phil Saxton. Pete was one of a kind. I believe Pete gave up as a trainer of boxers in order to devote his entire time into developing a family, and to them his love would be full and complete with his undivided attention. That's the way he operates—his only way. Phil and Pete remain close friends to this day.

Jersey Joe Walcott
in Two Parts

Part 1

Arnold Raymond Cream, the name sounds like it belongs to a Shakespearean actor, or to a proprietor of a large dairy farm. At age 16, Arnold, who was dirt poor, decided to become a professional boxer. It was the height of the Depression. America was down on its luck. There wasn't any work for millions of people. Families were lucky to eat once a day. Thousands were on "relief," that era's welfare system.

Arnold figured he could make a few bucks as a pro. He was tough and rugged; he'd follow some of his friends who were battling at local rings. First he'd have to change that name. As a youngster, he remembered his father always spoke about the Barbados Demon, Joe Walcott. The Demon was his dad's idol. Little Arnold liked the name, and so it became his ring moniker, Jersey Joe Walcott.

According to the record books, Joe started his pro career on September 9, 1930. That would make the youngster 16 years and 7 months old for his first fight. The record gives his date of birth as January 31, 1914, at Merchantville, New Jersey. Joe scored a one-round knockout over a fellow by the name of Cowboy Wallace, or Frank (Cowboy) Willis, depending on which name suits your fancy. Boxers' records were kept very lackadaisically if at all at the time. Main-event results were kept if the fight was considered important. The prelim results were dismissed half the time. Keeping records of pro boxing was in its infancy. Everlast sporting goods, the manufacturer of boxing equipment, started compiling fighters' records in the 1920s. Their little record books became quite popular (today they are collector's items). Other outfits took up the procedure. It was not until Nat Fleischer at the helm as the editor of *Ring* magazine that fighters' records were taken seriously and made more accurate. Nat researched back to the bare-knuckle days. Newspaper archives were of great help in gathering the results of fights long forgotten. The barber shop magazine *The Police Gazette* was a huge supplier of boxing write-ups and results.

In any event the records we have today on these old-time fighters are very good compared to the time they were first compiled. A lot of hard work from many people and different organizations brought about fruition. In my quest to find "more" on Jersey Joe, I searched my entire boxing library and then contacted Henry Hascup, a nationally known expert on sports, especially boxing. He had been researching Jersey Joe in the past and had already added lost fights to Joe's record. We both believe there are still fights Joe had that were not reported and never made the record books.

Jersey Joe Walcott weighed 135 pounds for the first fight and was paid $7.50 for his one-round win, good money in those days for a few minutes in the ring. Joe was used to "hard times," he being one of twelve children of a laborer. It came down to this: fights were hard to get, so the money wasn't easily available on a regular basis. Joe knew one doesn't get out of "hard times" so easily. In his first year he only had three fights. The next year, only one; the third year none. Joe worked any job he could get, from washing dishes to laying cement, anything to support his family. When Joe got a job that lasted a while, he'd stay with it until the pink slip. It made Joe a "sometimes" fighter. I believe he took some fights with no prior training, thus his spotty record. In years 1932, 1934, 1941, 1942, and 1943 Joe has no recorded fights. When in between jobs and with few fights, Joe had to apply for relief checks of $9.50 a week. The Walcott children were cold and hungry, and the coal bin was empty. Jersey Joe Walcott hired himself out as a sparring partner for the top contenders. During the 1930s, Joe Louis was in training for the first fight with Max Schmeling. The Joe Louis people hired Jersey Joe to spar with the great one at his Pompton Lakes, New Jersey, training camp. Jersey Joe lasted one day. He and his trainer claimed Jersey Joe floored the Bomber and easily outboxed him. After the workout, Walcott was paid off and told to leave. Louis's people denied it ever happened. Walcott insisted it did. More on this later.

Fighting on and off, Jersey Joe became a main eventer. His first knockout loss came at the hands of Al Ettore in eight rounds. Joe fought Billy Ketchell three times but could not get a win. Billy fought Walcott to two ten-round draws and then beat Joe on points in ten. Walcott scored a knockout over Phil Johnson. This fight is mentioned only because it would become a boxing oddity years later. The year was 1936. Walcott would kayo Phil Johnson's son in 1950. Harold Johnson would go on to win the Light Heavyweight Championship of the World. Only one other father-and-son case comes to mind. That would be Joe Frazier who defeated Joe Bugner by decision, and later his son Marvis Frazier also defeated Bugner on points.

Jersey Joe fought on, winning most but losing key bouts to Tiger Jack Fox twice, once by kayo. On February 12, 1940, Jersey Joe, 192 pounds, was knocked out by huge Abe Simon, 256 pounds, in six rounds at Newark, New Jersey. Joe gave Simon 64 pounds. Walcott retired; he went to work for the city of Camden as a garbage collector for the sanitation department.

Part 2

The Simon fight was the end of Jersey Joe's career Part 1. Enter onto the scene Felix Bocchicchio and Part 2. Felix was a boxing promoter, manager and all around boxing man. He had seen Walcott fight before and knew of his plight. He knew Walcott was a very sound heavyweight who had a muscular body without any fat. He also knew Joe was a real pro, a good counterpuncher who never wasted any unnecessary movement. He could knock a man cold with one punch if he landed right.

Felix sought out Joe and found him at home, unemployed again. Felix pleaded with Joe to try a comeback. He explained to Joe that with the right conditions in effect, the training, diet, steady fights, and most important to Joe, financial security for his family, he had more than the tools necessary to go all the way to the top of a now weak heavyweight division. Walcott was skeptical; he now had a wife and six children to feed, and that coal bin was still empty. He argued that in the past fights were few and far between. He needed steady employment.

Bocchicchio told Walcott to dismiss and forget his Part 1 resume.

Start fresh on a new Part 2 career. Felix filled that coal bin and promised Joe he'd be getting steady income. All he wanted from Joe was his all-out effort in a steady training regimen. Walcott could now put all his attention on boxing and *winning*. The meeting between these two men would make boxing history.

In his first fight on the comeback trail after four years and four months of inactivity, Walcott won an eight-round decision over club fighter Felix Del Paoli. Walcott was rusty, but it was a start. Six wins later he scored a huge upset over top-ranked, tough, Joe Baksi. They fought in Camden, New Jersey, Walcott's hometown, and Jersey Joe got the decision. The year was 1945, and back then all newspapers carried boxing results supplied by the Associated Press under the title "Last Night's Fight Results." That was the first time I ever heard of Jersey Joe Walcott. What an upset. Walcott would be heard of in every household in America before he was through. Boxing writers started giving Joe some ink, but many thought he was a flash in the pan. "The next contender he fights will probably flatten the old man," they crowed.

Walcott followed his Baksi win with kayos over veterans Johnny Denson and Steve Dudas. A D.Q. over Lee Q. Murray and a kayo over Curtis "Hatchetman" Sheppard, two top-ten heavies, cemented Walcott's presence among the best heavyweights in the world looking for a shot at the great Brown Bomber, Joe Louis.

In February of 1946, Walcott was matched with Jimmy Bivins in Jimmy's hometown of Cleveland, Ohio. Bivins was ranked number two under champ Louis and number-one contender Billy Conn, who were waiting to engage in their long-awaited return match. Bivins was so good he was recognized as "interim" champion while Louis was in the Armed Services during the war years. Going into the Walcott fight, Bivins was a huge favorite. He had won his last 26 fights over the best in the world. Bivins was at his peak and just 27 years old. *And Walcott upset him.* Jersey Joe had arrived at the top of the heap after 16 long years. It was Walcott's signature fight. Felix Bocchicchio was right—all Walcott needed was peace of mind. It brought out the best in this fighter who at long last could focus on boxing and boxing alone. As the great Teddy Atlas always claims, "seventy-five percent of this sport is mental." In Walcott's case it definitely was.

Now the writers had a field day. Who was this "old relic" from the early '30s who was tearing up the heavyweight division? They dubbed him the "Camden Methuselah." When they heard he had six kids, they called him "Pappy Joe."

The upset decision over Bivins won an immediate fight for Walcott in MSG. It would be his first appearance there. His opponent would be the very tricky, awkwardly clever Lee Oma. Joe would win a unanimous decision over Oma and would also pick up some of Oma's "style." The famous Walcott shift was borrowed from the elusive Oma's bag of tricks.

The Garden promoter had Walcott back a few months later and pitted him against power-punching Tommy Gomez, the "Jack Dempsey of the South." Gomez, a highly decorated war hero who was wounded at the Battle of the Bulge, would test Pappy Joe's chin. Walcott refused the test and laid Gomez low under the ropes in round three. Two weeks later Walcott would take on slick Joey Maxim and lose the decision in his own hometown. Elmer "Violent" Ray was next at MSG, and Joe lost again by split decision in a dull fight. It was the story of counterpuncher waiting on counterpuncher. Was this possibly the end for old Joe? Some people were saying old age finally got to Walcott.

Not by a long shot. Walcott came right back with decisions over Joey Maxim and Elmer Ray and then beat Maxim in the rubber match. While these fights were being fought, Joe Louis kayoed Tami Mauriello on September 18, 1946, after he had taken care of Billy Conn in their return encounter. Louis wanted to fight again in June of 1947 outdoors. Joe Baksi had taken over as number-one contender after wins over Freddie Mills and Bruce Woodcock, British light heavy and heavyweight champs, respectively. Both kayo wins were impressive, and Louis-Baksi looked like a good ballpark fight. Baksi had stopped Woodcock in April of 1947, and Louis was eager for a June fight at Yankee Stadium. Baksi, playing the "prima donna" role, insisted on a vacation first, visiting relatives in Europe. He would finance this vacation with a lucrative fight in Sweden with that country's champion, a real creampuff opponent for the vacationing Baksi. Joe *lost* the ten-round decision to Ollie Tandberg, an unknown in American rings. Baksi blew the ballpark fight for the title with Louis. One newspaper had a cartoon featuring Baksi standing in a corner with a dunce cap on—punishment for losing to a third-rater and losing a title shot. Louis, always an active champion, then turned his attention to Gus Lesnevich, the light heavy champ, who was doing well at the time. When offered the fight, Gus was honest to the fans and the promoter. He told Sol Strauss, the matchmaker, "I am not interested in a fight with Joe Louis." He knew it would be a mismatch.

There was no fight for Louis that summer of 1947. The reason given was there was not a worthy contender available—an insult to Jersey Joe Walcott who was the number-one contender after Baksi's loss. The Twentieth Century Sporting Club who promoted Louis fights and Louis's team always for some harebrained reason assumed that a black contender against Louis would not draw big at the gate. Louis wanted at least one fight in 1947 even if it had to be indoors in December at the Garden. To satisfy Joe Louis, his team and the MSG promoters agreed to use Jersey Joe vs. Joe Louis in a *ten-round exhibition fight.* That's how set they were in their belief that two blacks could not draw. It's almost unbelievable because Louis was managed by two black businessmen, and they did not want to give Walcott a shot at the title. Thank God the New York State athletic commission turned the exhibition gimmick down and demanded a 15-round title bout. It finally was agreed upon by all parties, so now they figured they had to beat the ballyhoo drums. So little was thought of Pappy Joe as a legitimate contender against Louis, the promoters figured they would have to build up Walcott with a deluge of publicity.

Publicists went to work. Walcott was written about every which way. In reality Walcott did not need any buildup: he was the real article. The writers kept calling him the old man, Pappy Joe, so older folks would get behind him, but if they checked, both Joes entered the ring at 33 years of age. The old story of Jersey Joe dropping Louis in training camp emerged again to let prospective ticket buyers believe Louis had a real challenge. This story was being milked to the point that one New York paper got a scoop when it was able to uncover and print photos of *Louis* doing the dropping of Walcott in spar sessions. Walcott would be only the second African American to challenge Joe Louis in 24 title defenses.

The theory of two blacks not being able to draw a large gate fell by the wayside when 18,000 fans packed the Garden and set a record for that arena. The gate was $225,000, very good figures for an affair that was originally booked as an exhibition. Ringside tickets sold at $30 a pop to see Pappy Joe, a 10–1 underdog not expected to last four rounds, with the Bomber. The only betting on the fight was how long the challenger could last. Joe Louis's drawing power was vastly underrated by his own team.

Well, boxing, being the king of sports that it is, again produced the unexpected. The "unworthy challenger" Jersey Joe Walcott punched Joe Louis dizzy, especially in the first round, flooring him for a two count and in the fourth round dropping the Bomber for a seven count. The fans were going crazy. The Garden was rocking. Some fans were stunned with disbelief. Others expecting one of the biggest upsets in boxing history. Static electricity was in the air as the fight continued round after round. Walcott with a hit-and-run-and-circle was befuddling the ever-advancing champion. He was also using the shift he learned from Lee Oma to further confuse Louis.

The champion's left eye was closing, he was bleeding from the nose, his face was puffed and his left ear was sprouting cauliflower going into the 15th and final round. Louis had pushed the fight all the way, but most thought he had lost by the final bell. In fact Louis himself thought he lost. He left the ring before the decision was announced. He had to be called back into the ring to hear that he had *won a split decision* and retained his crown for the 24th time. Pandemonium broke loose at Madison Square Garden with the announcement of the officials' cards. Judge Marty Monroe gave nine rounds to Louis, six to Walcott. Referee Ruby Goldstein had it seven to six, Walcott. Judge Frank Forbes had it 8–6–1, Louis, for the split. A crescendo of boos and Bronx cheers drowned out Harry Borough, the ring announcer. The Garden was a complete madhouse. The next day the papers were full of the "robbery." *Police Gazette* named Jersey Joe Walcott their heavyweight champion. People demanded a return fight. Walcott had done himself proud and every Jerseyite the same. The Joe Louis–Jersey Joe Walcott fight would go down in boxing history as one of the top heavyweight fights of all time. It was not an all-out barnburner by any means, but it was a tactical fight, with the lowly underdog making the great champion look downright bad, putting him in a position the fans had never seen him in before as a titleholder. The fight public was in love with this old warrior, the family man with a wife and six kids. Yankee Stadium, here comes Jersey Joe Walcott.

Fight fans were hyped up and salivating at the mouth waiting for the Louis-Walcott return bout. They gave a second look at Jersey Joe's accomplishments. He could stand with the best punchers, such as Tommy Gomez, Curtis Sheppard and Elmer Ray, and kayo them. He outboxed the boxing master Joey Maxim. Above all he floored Joe Louis *twice*, the biggest puncher of all. Many people figured Jersey Joe would become the next champion come June 25, 1948.

At the time I saw Joe Louis in training, I was 15 years old. I remember vividly watching this man go through his paces. It was like seeing a monarch grace his throne room. Everyone was in awe of this great fighter who dominated the heavyweights for 11 years as their champion. His every move was fluid and natural. His trainer and cornermen worked around him as a unit, reminiscent of a race car pulling into a pit stop at the Indianapolis 500—efficient, precise and all caring deeply for *their* car. So it was with Louis and his corner at Pompton Lakes training camp before the second Walcott fight.

His spar mates were selected for their ability to imitate Walcott's style, which they did and were good at. Louis's modus operandi was plainly seen by onlookers as a "seek and destroy" mission. Louis took on four spar mates that beautiful Sunday afternoon. Some had fear in their eyes, and their body language supported that fear. They hotfooted around that ring with the Brown Bomber in hot pursuit. Louis in a very serious mood dropped each one of them in their two-round sessions. In each case Joe backed off after scoring the knockdowns and let each man finish. *Awesome.* Walcott was in for a rough night come June. Joe Louis was a man on the warpath. He wanted revenge on the man who degraded him and made him look so ordinary and totally confused at Madison Square Garden six months past.

The second Louis vs. Walcott fight was held at Yankee Stadium in June of 1948. The crowd was estimated at 45,000, the gate $740,000. Joe Louis came in at 213½ to the challenger's 194¾. Joe Louis was an 11–5 favorite, a far cry from the 10–1 favorite in their first fight. The referee was Frank Fullam.

Pappy Joe started right off as he continued his torturous hit-and-run assault he used in their first fight. He kept his distance, hitting and getting out of range while keeping Louis off balance. He'd launch his big sneak right hand periodically to keep Louis on the cautious side, which would give Pappy Joe the time he needed to outbox Louis. That right had dropped Louis *twice* last fight and already had him down here in the third round for a one count in this the second fight. Louis learned to respect Walcott's right hand. He couldn't just walk right through Walcott. He had to catch Walcott when he made a mistake with a wrong move. Louis was starting to get desperate. The rounds were slipping away, and so was his precious championship. Louis and his corner were tense as the championship rounds, the 11th through 15th, approached. He had to nail this elusive challenger.

Coming out for the 11th round, Walcott got cocky and started to take chances. He was ahead on both judges' scorecards. Jersey Joe figured he was "flying home" to the world title. That's when the roof caved in. Louis finally found what he was looking for in 26 rounds of fighting this brash contender. A blistering right hand followed by a huge right uppercut stunned Walcott. Louis finished him with a two-fisted attack. Pappy Joe took the full ten count at 2:56 of the 11th round. The kayo marked Louis's 25th defense and 22nd kayo in his title reign. When Joe Louis hurt an opponent, that was it. He was one of the greatest finishers ever in heavyweight history.

Poor Jersey Joe, so near yet so very far. The crown had eluded him twice now. Joe Louis must have seen the handwriting on the wall. He just finished two hectic struggles with Walcott and was lucky to still be champion. Louis announced his retirement as undefeated champion on March 1, 1949.

In June of that year, the NBA decided to match the number-one contender Ezzard Charles vs. Jersey Joe Walcott for their version of the heavyweight title. Walcott lost the unanimous decision to the Cincinnati Cobra at Comiskey Park, Chicago. It was Pappy Joe's third attempt to grab that crown. He would fight on.

Ezzard Charles would defeat Joe Louis, who was attempting a comeback, to gain universal recognition as heavyweight champion in September of 1950. Ezzard was a busy titleholder and offered Jersey Joe another shot at the crown. Their fight was almost a carbon copy of their first, with Charles again winning a unanimous decision. The fight was held in Detroit. Pappy Joe had his fourth crack at the title that was always out of his reach. The year 1951.

Why in the world would Ezzard Charles and his team decide to fight Jersey Joe Walcott a third time after winning two unanimous decisions over the Camden Methuselah? Ezz had cleaned up the division but was still looking for work. He and his brain trust must have figured, let's recycle Pappy Joe again. It'll be another easy defense, and Walcott was still respected among the fans. Their first two fights weren't great, but they held fan interest. Why not? It will be another payday. *Wrong, dead wrong.* In his 37th round of boxing against Ezz, which would make it the seventh round in this their third clash, Walcott landed as beautiful a left hook as anyone ever saw. Only Ezz never seen it. He caught it flush on the jaw, and it dropped the champion like a felled ox. Ezz was counted out in a terrific upset. Boxing experts could only surmise that the old Wily Methuselah had finally figured Ezz out and timed him for that smashing hook. Jersey Joe was finally heavyweight champion of the world. He won it on a record fifth attempt. The time was 55 seconds of the seventh round. *Ring* magazine named it fight of the year for 1951. At age 37, Pappy Joe was the oldest man ever to win that title. It was also the first heavyweight title fight ever held in Pittsburgh. The date was July 18, 1951. One thousand Camdenites surrounded Walcott's modest home at 1020 Cooper Street to extend their congratulations and share the joy with the Walcott family. The former garbageman came back to Camden in a limousine.

Jersey Joe made older Americans feel great. It was a fine feeling to see a man of his age hold the most precious prize in sports. He was visioned as a second "Cinderella Man." Like the original, Joe was a family man, a New Jerseyite, an underdog on a comeback. He toiled at many jobs and had to accept welfare, as did James J. Braddock before him. Jersey Joe Walcott and James J. Braddock in their time of desperation both turned to the only sport that gave everyone a chance back in those years—Boxing.

It did not turn them away; it only made it possible for both men to retain their self-respect. It wasn't an easy road they were offered. It called for deep dedication. They would have to sweat blood and tears and work their muscles sore. But if they were game and sincere they could make a go of it. Boxing cared little of their skin colors. Braddock was Irish-American; Walcott, African American. Both were welcome to win boxing's biggest prize, the Heavyweight Championship of the World. And by God they *did*. Both became rich and famous.

A year after kayoing Ezzard, Pappy Joe gave him a return bout. This would be their fourth meeting. The fight would be held in Philadelphia.

This time Walcott would win the unanimous decision in 15 rounds, with scores of 9–6, 8–7, and 7–6–2. Many boxing fans and writers thought Ezzard had won, but no one hollered too loud because Ezz did not do enough to warrant taking the title from the champion.

Three months later Jersey Joe would probably fight the greatest fight of his career. He would take on his number-one contender, the undefeated Brockton Blockbuster, Rocky Marciano.

From the time the fight was signed till the moment they stepped into the ring, Walcott was extremely confident. The old consummate pro that he was, he could not see himself losing to Marciano. In Joe's eyes, Rocky was a bumbling, awkward and clumsy overhyped Golden Glove novice wild swinger. He would burst the Marciano bubble. Walcott told newsmen, "Write this in the paper. He can't fight. If I don't lick him, take my name out of the record books." Jersey Joe could not mentally accept Rocky as a threat. He would go right out there and crush that Rock and prove himself right. That's what made it the great fight it was, another example of Teddy Atlas's theory on the mental state of pugilists going into a fight.

The fight was set for September 23, 1952, at Municipal Stadium, Philadelphia. Fifteen rounds or less. Walcott answered the first-round bell with an ardor about himself of half disdain and half cockiness toward his challenger. He set out to destroy Rocky. The first minute and a half, Rocky was still looking to land. A sudden left hook with terrific power dropped the Rock. The first knockdown of his career. A three count. Rocky was able to last out the round. Walcott was flying high. He knew he would annihilate this crude club fighter. Walcott abandoned the style made famous in the two Louis fights. He set down to "power punching." He would fight this Brockton Blockbuster. The result was the best heavyweight title fight ever. They blazed away at each other with knockout punches filling the air. Each being rocked as the rounds moved on. Marciano was staggered in the 5th through 11th and 12th rounds. Going into the 13th round, the bridge of Rocky's nose was cut and he had a scalp wound. Walcott had a one-and-a-half-inch cut over his left eye. He seemed to be "flying home" again. He was way out front. Rocky and his corner knew the only way the Rock could win was by kayo.

This furious battle came to an abrupt end at 42 seconds of the 13th round. One short brutal right hand exploded on Pappy Joe's jaw. He went down for the full count, his title *gone*. Forty thousand fans saw a classic. Many experts say that Rocky's punch was the hardest and most perfect right cross ever thrown in boxing. Rocky definitely needed that knockout to win. Referee Taggert had it 7–4–1, Judge Clayton 8–4 and Judge Tomasco 7–5, all for Walcott. If the fight was held with today's rules, Walcott would have retained his title. Rocky would not have become the only undefeated heavyweight champ in history. This writer's opinion is that 15 rounds should apply to all title fights. The 12-round system was brought in only to please TV time limits. Also trashed should be the three-knockdown rule, which has soiled many good fights.

In any case the fight was a true classic. It heaped much glory on both battlers and boxing. Walcott fought his heart out and earned the respect of many in his "victory in defeat" effort. There had to be a rematch.

It would take place on May 15, 1953, at Chicago Stadium. Walcott would again be challenging for a record *sixth* time. Marciano came in a 3–1 favorite. At two minutes 25 seconds of round one the fight was over.

Referee Frank Sikora counted out Jersey Joe after Rocky landed a smashing right hand to Joe's jaw. Naturally press and fans alike didn't like the quick ending. There were many questions, but few answers were given. *Ring* magazine wrote, "Did old age finally catch up with the Methuselah?" Many people believed Walcott was in reality at least 44 years old. Boxing writers and experts did not like Walcott's looks at any time after the match was made. He looked bad in training. At the weigh-in he looked listless. No fire. Some said he was going to his execution. He came into the fight drawn and worried. Did he quit? Many think he did. My opinion: they are the same experts who damned Joe before the first Louis fight, claiming he wouldn't last four rounds, the very same flunkies that gave Pappy Joe no chance in his third fight in which he laid Ezzard Charles low. Those same people who went negative on Walcott were praising him a few months earlier on his game and gallant stand against the Rock. I go with Walcott and referee Frank Sikora, when he said, "Don't let anyone tell you Walcott didn't get hit. Marciano really started the knockout with a right under the heart. Next came the left hook high on the cheek, and then Rocky really drilled him with a terrific right. It may not have shown on TV, but believe me, I was the closest man seeing that punch, and it was a knockout punch." The so-called experts with their criticism of Walcott took away from both fighters, by questioning an old warrior's brave heart and degrading a great win for Marciano.

This writer believes Walcott left it all in that great first fight in Philly. He came into the second Marciano fight with newfound respect for his opponent. He wasn't as pumped up as he was mentally for that first fight. The disgruntled fans in time would agree. Jersey Joe gave it his all. Even steel has its "metal fatigue" point when it will break. Joe's came at 2:25 of round one. There is an end to everything. It was his last fight. The Camden Methuselah was finally finished.

After his retirement from boxing, Pappy Joe remained as always a goodwill ambassador for our sport. Jersey Joe helped politicians in their campaigns, which enabled him to be appointed as New Jersey State boxing commissioner. He did a stint as county sheriff along with guest referee assignments, speaking engagements, etc. He did well. I recall the night I attended the Chuck Wepner–Tommy Sheehan fight in Kearny, New Jersey. Pappy Joe was introduced in the ring, and I never saw a fighter get such a standing ovation as he did. Everyone, I mean *everyone*, stood for at least five minutes applauding the old gladiator. Joe kept waving to the crowd, and the length of the applause got him totally embarrassed. He looked great; he couldn't have been much over his fighting weight. And this was May 6, 1976, 23 years after his last fight. One couldn't help thinking those fans that night in Kearny knew that this man had floored Joe Louis *three times*, Rocky Marciano once, and knocked out Ezzard Charles, three all-time greats. In memories of Walcott one cannot forget his quote to the press when asked about his thoughts of Muhammad Ali as the greatest heavyweight champion ever: "He may be just what he says he is, the greatest." I've never heard any other former heavyweight champ say that. Their usual answer is always in their favor or someone from their era.

As long as boxing exists, Walcott will be remembered as the man who against all odds never gave up in his quest to accomplish his lifetime goal, that being to win the Heavyweight Championship of the World. In five *unprecedented* attempts, his never-ending will prevailed, and Jersey Joe Walcott stood alone above all contenders. The sparring partner for hire who would be king. Arnold Raymond Cream, aka Jersey Joe Walcott, passed away on February 25, 1994, at age eighty.

Jersey Joe's Greatest Fights

1. Ezzard Charles W 15
2. Ezzard Charles KO 7
3. Harold Johnson KO 3
4. Joey Maxim W 10
5. Tommy Gomez KO 3
6. Lee Oma W 10
7. Jimmy Bivins W 10
8. Curtis Sheppard KO 10
9. Steve Dudas KO 5
10. Joe Baksi W 10
11. Elmer Ray KO 3

Near Yet Oh So Far

Joe Louis L 15
Rocky Marciano KO by 13

The Irvington Milkman: Charley Fusari, New Jersey's Golden Boy

It would be impossible to write about New Jersey boxing and the great boxers the state produced and not include the Irvington Milkman—Charley Fusari. He never won a championship, but if ever there was a Golden Boy he was *it*. He had Hollywood leading-man good looks. This handsome blond Italian-American was very popular with the fans. Men were won over to him by his power punches plus his will to win, along with large amounts of courage and heart. Charley gave 100 percent of himself every time he stepped through the ropes. Never in a dull fight. The women fans just liked to look at him. Charley was a welterweight, slim yet well muscled for his frame. The 147-pounder always appeared in public well dressed and neat in appearance. We the fans saw him as soft-spoken, well behaved, and very articulate. He treated his fans with respect as he did his opponents. There was no braggart or loud foul-mouth behavior that sorrowfully we see in some of today's superstars. Charley was down to earth, and he became Jersey's star. Even when his career hit the heights, Charley never got a swelled head. The young man had class and charisma. He became a role model to young fighters coming up.

This writer never knew Fusari personally, nor have I interviewed him. I write this sketch of him as his fan who followed his career from the first time I ever heard of him. All a loyal fan can learn of his hero is to attend his fights when and if possible. Catch his TV fights. Read all you can find on him. If possible visit his training camp and of course keep rooting for him. I can only offer the reader the things I learned about Charley's boxing career. His personal life aside, we will focus on only the boxing side that we know.

We do know Charley was born in Alcamo, Sicily, Italy, in 1924. He came to America at a very young age. His family settled in Irvington, New Jersey. Charley had an older brother who began boxing, and Charley took up after him. Tommy Fusari started fighting professionally at the New Jersey clubs on the undercards. Charley entered the amateur ranks briefly and then turned pro in May of 1944 at age 18. Older brother Tommy's career fizzled while Charley's caught on. Young Charley had a job on a milk delivery truck and claimed his good conditioning came from the many thousands of stairs he'd climbed and the running involved in delivering the bottles of milk. This caught on with boxing writers, and the name Irvington Milkman was born.

As a youngster of 12, I remember vividly the year 1945. I kept seeing fight posters around town. Some were put in store and bar windows. Others were nailed to telephone poles or tacked onto nonresidential buildings. To explain their existence, one had to know our town, Elizabeth, New Jersey. We had a local promoter; his name was George "Korn" Kobb. He should be enshrined in the Boxing Hall of Fame. He made Elizabeth a boxing town and developed on his boxing cards some of the great names of the day. Kobb ran weekly fights at the Elizabeth Armory and at Twin City Bowl on the Newark Elizabeth city line. Before that he had run shows at tiny Scott Hall in downtown Elizabeth. Some bright stars got their start at Scott Hall such as Rocky Graziano, Joe Baksi, Freddy Archer, Freddy Russo, Frankie Duane, Clint Miller, etc., etc.

Getting back to the posters, the residents were used to seeing them from all the boxing activity we had. The aforementioned names were familiar to all. Kobb was responsible for distributing the posters all over town. They were his main source of advertising his fight cards. In 1945, I noticed a new name on the posters, one I couldn't pronounce. *Fusari.* If you are not familiar with fight posters, you would find them to be a 24" × 20" cardboard. Across the top would be the locale and date of the fight. Below this would be the favorite's name in large bold red letters. The name below on the bottom would always be in black. The name in black would be the underdog. Some posters would also have the photo of each fighter in his best fighting pose. Under the large name in black was the line "other star bouts," which would start with the semifinal. It would be names like Johnny "Red" DeFazio of Bayonne vs. Tommy Kaczmerek of Elizabeth. Names for the other bouts on the card were something like Joey Gabrielle of Orange vs. Charley McGarry of Rahway. Maybe names like Tic Mollozzi of Elizabeth vs. Eldred "Fox" Williams of New York would be mentioned fighting the four-rounders on the card. Other names you might find on these posters who fought the undercards were well known to the fans, men like Tony Rose, Johnny Darby, Lenny LaBrutta, Birdie Loffa, Tommy Parks, Butch Charles, Freddy Hermann, etc. All good fighters who came to *fight*. Truly a fight fan's bonanza.

None of these guys ever came into the ring dressed like clowns or wrestlers as some fighters do today. I noticed the Fusari name was always in red, the favorite. In fine print under his name it would say "Undefeated Irvington Sensation." I was hooked. I became a fan. I asked some adults how they would pronounce that name. One bright guy told me to accent the U and then give the I an E sound. It worked, and the name was easy to pronounce thereafter.

That year, 1945, the Fusari name was tops over fighters like Lou Miller, Pat Scanlon, Pat Demers and Joey Peralta. Charley was making it big with win after win. They even started putting posters in Elizabeth of Charley's fights that were held in Newark. The names in black were getting to be well known, but Charley was always on top in his favorite color, red. I didn't know then, but those posters would become collector's items in future years. The main thing with Fusari was his win streak. It reminded me of the weekly serial at the movie theater. They had 15 chapters. Each week the hero, let's say the Green Hornet, was in distress at the end of the chapter. It was only fitting for the kids to return next Saturday to see if the Green One survived.

Good business, because the Hornet would again be ready for his demise this week also. It went on for 15 chapters; that way the movie house was filled to capacity each Saturday.

So it was with Charley Fusari. We would all be tuned in to see if he would remain undefeated, taking on foe after foe. When he fought out of town, we kids were after the next day's afternoon edition of the newspaper. And Charley, he was great. He kept it going. It's incredible, compared to today's standards, but check the record books if you are a nonbeliever. Fusari fought *22* times in 1945. His streak was 32 straight at year's end. Fights were available, and they fought them in those days. With the arrival of Fusari on the fistic scene, it couldn't have been better timing. TV was becoming immensely popular. In Elizabeth, on the avenue at evening time, appliance stores would set up and turn on a TV in the window when closing for the night. At each store it was common to see groups of people standing on the sidewalk in all kinds of weather watching the TV until the programs went off the air for the night. The playing of the National Anthem signified the station was through for the evening, thereby dispersing the crowd.

I recall seeing my first TV fight in July 1945, standing outside a local tavern, looking at the set through a side screen door. My friends and I were considered too young to be left inside the bar. The tavern was packed with fans, there to see the Friday night fights from MSG in New York City. The bar owners who could afford a large TV set had found a goldmine in the fights. A good set went for big bucks then and was out of reach for most blue-collar folks. However, they could afford to nurse a few beers while enjoying the fights. From our position on the sidewalk, we picked a bummer of a fight to watch. In a clash of styles, Freddy Russo of Rahway, New Jersey, lost a dreary ten-rounder to Sal Bartolo, partial featherweight champion, by unanimous decision. Undefeated Russo lost his first fight.

Boxing being the easiest of all sports to televise because the "playing field" is so small and stationery, it became the darling of the networks. Fights started being televised six nights a week in the next few years. TV sets were getting easier to purchase by the working class. With it, boxing boomed.

Nineteen forty-six was Fusari's breakout year. He got his first St. Nicholas Arena main event. St. Nick's was the Garden's farm club. Charley took on old vet Maxie Berger and walked away with the decision. He was called back a few months later to defeat Humberto Zavala, a rugged pug who tested all the young rookies. Charley made it 39 straight.

With his win streak in tact and his pleasing wins over Berger and Zavala, the promoters began looking to Freddy Archer as Fusari's next opponent. Freddy was a top welterweight for years, and he beat some of the best, such as two wins over Beau Jack and also a decision over Ike Williams. Enough said. Archer was also a Newark, New Jersey, boy, a neighbor to Irvington Charley. A match between the two would fill Ruppert Stadium and supply the acid test to the all-winning Fusari. Charley would be going after his win in Archer.

The fight was a blowout. Fusari simply blew poor Freddy out of the ring. Charley came out of his corner with the opening bell and showered Archer with knockout punches, showing no respect at all for the highly regarded Newark fighter. Archer was sent crashing to the canvas three times in the first round. Somehow he managed to last out the round only to take a severe pasting until he was floored again in the sixth round. Archer's corner did not let him answer the seventh-round bell. It was Fusari's biggest win. His next stop, MSG.

The wheels were turning for a match with the Garfield Gunner, Tippy Larkin, my favorite fighter. I really hated to see this match made. I figured Larkin would ruin a terrific prospect. The fight was set for December 13, 1946. Larkin pulled out of the match and Chuck Taylor would be his substitute. Taylor boasted two wins over Archer and had already fought two main events at the Garden. Fusari would have his hands full. For three rounds it looked that way, with Fusari taking a pounding. Taylor was winning easily, and then Charley got hot. He started to bang Taylor all over the ring, landing one bomb after another. Taylor couldn't come out for the seventh. Charley had a kayo for his 44th straight and his first main event in the Garden. The postponement of the Larkin fight and the convincing win over sub Chuck Taylor made the Larkin-Fusari fight a sellout for the Garden when it was finally put on in February 1947.

Larkin came into the ring a huge favorite. He had over 100 victories on his ledger and loads of experience over the 21-year-old blond bomber. A crowd of over 18,000 showed up for a gross gate of over $115,000, huge for the times. Charley not only looked like a golden boy; he was one.

Charley and his brain trust must have looked at it this way. It was impossible to outpoint Tippy Larkin. Their only chance was to throw the right-hand bomb over and over and take charge. That's exactly what Fusari did. He came out swinging at the first-round bell. Midway through the round he floored Larkin for a six count. From there on until the end it was a rout. Tippy would be dropped again in the second, seventh, and twice in the ninth before referee Arthur Donovan stopped the fight. Charley had his 45th straight win and was ranked number two after Tommy Bell for Sugar Ray Robinson's welterweight title. The Garden had a new drawing card, the best since Beau Jack and Rocky Graziano. Charley made the *Ring* magazine cover for June 1947, with the caption, "Charley Fusari Undefeated New Jersey Welterweight Sensation New Contender for Ray Robinson's Title."

Garden officials put the new drawing card to work just four months later. Charley was matched against another Garden favorite, Tough Tony Pellone. Tony was a well-respected opponent. He had some very good wins under his belt, and it was thought he'd give the Golden Boy a real battle. Tony was not a hard puncher, and a lot of people figured Charley could just walk through him. They overlooked the fact of just how tough Tony was. He was a brawler who threw punches in bunches, and he knew what he was doing inside them ropes. Tony had victories over Bob Montgomery, Billy Graham, and Paddy Young, among others. Tony was an expert at stealing rounds. Fight buffs called him Tony "Split Decision" Pellone.

It was uncanny the way he'd "shoe-shine," as Teddy Atlas would say. The shoe shine would come into play near the ending of any close round. Tony would unload a bunch of these harmless-type punches to finish the round in an attempt to sway the judges, although his opponent fought the entire round landing the harder and cleaner punches, as Charley did. It's only human nature to recall the last furious rally of the round, and some judges and fans fell for it. I believe that's what brought Charley his first defeat.

On June 13, 1947, Charley Fusari's streak was ended at 45 straight. His 46th fight spelled disaster for the Blond Bomber. Some records record 48 straight for Fusari. Take your pick. The fact remains, Charley never fought such a tough, cagey guy like Pellone before. Charley's right-hand bombs only shook Pellone but didn't drop him. Tony, with his punch-in-bunch roughhouse style had Charley baffled in this tough Garden bout. Charley, who was installed by the gamblers as a 12–5 favorite, started swelling around the left eye by the end of the fifth round. Fusari took his first loss like the pro that he was and called Pellone "tough." The scoring was judge Jack O'Sullivan, 5–4–1, Fusari; judge Marty Monroe, 6–4, Pellone; and referee Arthur Donovan, 6–3–1, Pellone. So again Tony lived up to his nickname, "Split Decision." Pellone fought the fight he had to fight, and it was one of his best efforts. In any event, both fighters fought hard and well.

The Garden bigwigs were stunned by Charley's loss. They had to get Fusari back on track. Their new drawing card had to regain lost prestige. Fusari fans felt bad because Charley had worked so damn hard to get to the top and the bigger money, only to lose such a close one. Everyone involved with the matchmaking agreed Fusari needed some immediate wins to take the sting out of the Pellone loss.

A little over a month later, Charley was back in the Garden paired with Eddie Giosa. Boxing buffs couldn't understand why Giosa was chosen. He had a style almost a carbon copy of Pellone's. If they wanted to get Charley back on the winning side, their selection of Giosa was in error. Maybe Fusari's recent smashing kayo victories had the matchmaker seeing through rose-colored glasses.

The fight with Giosa was a nip-and-tuck, slam-bang affair. Steady Eddie was slipping and sliding, ducking and countering, in most likely the fight of his life. He bullied and tried to keep Charley off stride. The writers called it the best fight of the season, which was halfway into the yearly schedule. Little Eddie Giosa came into the Garden ring a 5–17 underdog. Charley was pegged at 2–1 to score a kayo. Giosa being shorter and lighter in weight, it certainly looked like a mismatch.

The fight drew the smallest turnout of the year. Giosa wasn't given a chance, and the tickets didn't sell. He had earned the fight by being a consistent winner in the smaller New York City clubs the past year. The fans that did show up at the Garden were in for a huge surprise. "Upset." Giosa came to fight, and fight he did. The small crowd immediately got behind the underdog as boxing fans usually do. They rooted little Eddie all the way in for his victory. Referee Arthur Donovan had it 5–5 in rounds and 12 points to 12 for a *draw*. Judge Tom Guilhoyle had it 5–5 in rounds with 10–9 in points for Giosa. Judge Frank Forbes had it 5–4–1, Giosa. How close can you get?

Two losses in a row set Fusari back big time. People wondered, was he a flash in the pan? A bright shooting star that burned out so soon and completely? We all would find out soon enough. The heart and determination of this fighter would now be tested. Would he feel sorry for himself and lay down, or would he stand up and be counted? The best of Charley Fusari was yet to come. That's what made it a pleasure to follow this Golden Boy's career.

The Pellone and Giosa losses jolted Charley's fans back to the world of reality. With each KO win he had scored, some people, including boxing writers, were getting carried away with visions of Charley defeating the impossible-to-defeat Sugar Ray Robinson. In all probability Fusari's right hand fascinated them into that belief.

Charley was handled by the Marsillo brothers. Vic was his manager, and a very good one by the way. He had the right connections and the know-how to take Fusari to the heights. Vic's brother Tony was a good trainer. With the Marsillo brothers and Charley's punch and will to win, I couldn't see him out of the limelight for any length of time. As a fan, about this time I received a huge lift as far as Charley's ability was concerned. One evening while watching fighters train at the local gym, I had the pleasure of meeting Butch Charles. This retired fighter was pointed out to me by a trainer who knew I was a Fusari fan. I walked up to Butch and asked him if what the trainer had told me was true. The trainer (Tony Orlando) claimed Butch had fought and lost twice to Fusari. Butch Charles admitted he lost two six-round decisions to Fusari. He also claimed to have fought and beat Paddy DeMarco. (DeMarco was destined to become lightweight champion of the world.) I asked Butch what he thought of Fusari. He claimed Charley was a very good puncher, especially with "that right hand." "If Fusari stays dedicated and listens to his trainers, he can't miss." I was surprised by his comments. Usually when you talk to a fighter about his losses, they almost always claim they were robbed or the ref had it in for them, etc., etc. Not Butch Charles, he simply answered my questions, never claiming anything to benefit himself or make excuses for the losses. He praised his opponent. Butch Charles showed class. His comments picked me up out of the doldrums from any subconscious thoughts that Fusari couldn't come back.

A month after the Giosa loss, Fusari was back at MSG, this time against a former service champion who won an all–Army title while overseas, Joe DiMartino. After his discharge, Joe fought mainly in the New England area, winning some, losing some, until he finally got a match with a big name—the former welterweight champion of the world Marty Servo. Marty was on a comeback after relinquishing the title. DiMartino grabbed the "gold ring" and scored a stunning kayo over the bewildered ex-champ. When you get the gold ring, you always get a big-money reward. For Joe it was a Fusari bout in the Garden. DiMartino's first garden main event was a disaster. Either he choked or suffered the fate of so many first-time main-eventers in boxing's "Punch Palace"— Gardenitus. Fusari simply slammed Joe around like a beach ball.

DiMartino wasn't in the fight at all. The win did nothing to enhance Charley's prestige. It went into the books as a four-round kayo win for Fusari, best to be forgotten.

Vic Marsillo decided to take his charge to the New England area for further seasoning and hopefully some impressive wins in a series of fights against other styles, the more difficult the better. Charley was known to have an "awkwardly clever style," along with a right-hand bomb. So some good fights were at hand for Fusari, and also a learning process that would pay off big in Charley's future. Marsillo knew exactly what he was doing.

Now the reader must grasp the situation as it was in late 1947 and all of 1948. Here was this young handsome kid. A fan favorite. A large drawing card who was still a leading contender for the title, in short a golden boy ready to fight local boys in their hometowns. These fighters whom Charley would be fighting were never rated, never fought for big money. Grant you, they were good; only they never got the right breaks. Here was their chance to fight a big name. They simply got ready for the fight of their lives. They trained like Rocky Balboa and fought like they never had before. If they caught the gold ring as DiMartino did against Servo, they would be rewarded with all the things a top fighter got in those days—a money bout and a chance to be rated in the top ten.

Charley caught hell in most of his next dozen fights. He had to fight for his life for small purses. He did get the experience, and the wins kept him rated among the top ten. He would battle his way back to Madison Square Garden for some money fights. His first fight after the lackluster DiMartino win was a bout with Johnny Cesario, a very slick boxer, not nationally known but well thought of in New England rings. Charley fought him in Boston to a very hard-fought draw. Charley's brain trust thought he was robbed and demanded a return bout, only this time in Newark, New Jersey, Charley's turf. Charley lost in an upset in the return. Cesario caught the gold ring, fought the two best fights of his career, became nationally known, rated, and got more than a few TV fights for good money. Charley went back to Boston to kayo Gus "Pell" Mell, another New Englander, and then went right back to Boston and lost to Al "Red" Priest in a torrid ten-rounder. Priest was a good fighter, but only known by hard-core boxing fans and his Boston faithful. Now he was known throughout the boxing world at Fusari's expense. He too had caught the gold ring. Two months later Charley reversed the tables right there in Boston. And so it went. Charley came back to my hometown for fights with Laurie Buxton and Ruby Kessler. Both were average to good club fighters who were believed to be able to give Charley good workouts. They both fought the best fight of their careers. Everything to gain and nothing to lose. Charley had to fight like hell to take down both decisions. The Fusari vs. Kessler fight set an all-time record in money and attendance for promoter George "Korn" Kobb at Twin City Bowl. I had the pleasure of attending both fights, and Kobb outdid himself with the Fusari-Kessler brawl. Twin City Bowl was packed. Fans were turned away. At least 20 people crawled up on the dressing-room roof. They perched there to watch the fights to the dismay of the police who tried to get them down, but gave up trying when the prelims started. It was lucky that the roof was able to hold up under all that weight, thus avoiding a horrific accident.

Fusari and Kessler was a huge success, both boys very popular with Elizabeth fans. When I think back, George Kobb brought so many good fighters to Elizabeth. Recalled are Sugar Ray Robinson (three times), Beau Jack, Willie Pep, Arturo Godoy, Melio Bettina, Tami Mauriello, Fritzi Zivic, Tommy Bell, and so many others too numerous to mention. Kobb's shows were always well-contested bouts available to the fans at down-to-earth prices.

Charley was becoming a finished fighter, gaining mucho experience in these competitive fights. He finished 1948 with a kayo in Boston and two knockouts in Jersey City over Tony Riccio, the tough Bayonne battler, and a second kayo win over Tippy Larkin, his old foeman.

It was now 1949, Charley's best year. He started with a ten-round win over little-known Frankie Palermo at the Mosque Theatre in Newark, New Jersey. A barnburner, Palermo was determined to come away with an upset win. Charley had to climb off the floor to win this one. I attended the fight, and it was worth every penny of the $1.50 I paid for my ticket. Kobb was branching out into Newark for this one.

Charley was now through with school. His next bout would be where he belonged, back at Madison Square Garden. Six weeks after Palermo, he would take on the highly regarded Rocky Castellani. Charley had fought his way back into the Garden main bout by fighting a host of rough, tough determined fighters.

I like to call the Castellani fight one of the top wins of Charley's career. Rocky was a complete fighter. He was a very good boxer, and he could punch; very tricky and ring wise was he. Rocky was installed the favorite at 7–5. He was the "Rookie of the Year" for 1948 and had a four-pound pull in the weights—Fusari 147½ to Rocky's 151¼. His punch put Fusari down right off the bat in the first round. Charley survived the round and fought uphill for the remainder of the pleasing fight and walked off with the unanimous decision. Rocky Castellani was the best fighter Charley had defeated up to this point in his career, Rocky being young, strong and able. I'm not forgetting Tippy Larkin. Larkin was in the twilight of his long career when he first fought the young Fusari, but it too was a big win for Charley.

As Fusari was battling his way back to the big time, another young welterweight was making huge waves out in the Midwest. His name was Vince Foster; he was managed by the affable Jack Hurley and could punch like a mule kick. His style was exactly like Rocky Graziano's. With a string of kayos behind him, Hurley brought Foster to New York. Foster was easy to sell. He had youthful good looks and a muscular body with an all-out killer style. The Garden matchmakers put him in a semifinal bout against fan favorite Nick Mistovich, a real tough guy. Both boys went at it hammer and tong, with Foster winning the decision. The fans loved this kid, who was billed as of Irish–American Indian heritage. The Indian part of it was true; his family lived on a Midwest reservation, and he had attended Indian schools. That blond hair had to be the Irish in him. The fighting instincts could be attributed to both nationalities, both being noted for ferocious fighting qualities. The Garden was quick to match this dynamo with Tough Tony Pellone. Tony fought many main bouts in the Garden. Although he took on the best, like Ike Williams, Kid Gavilan, Tony Janiro, Billy Graham, and Gharley Fusari, he was never kayoed there. This kid Foster would change all that. Pellone was installed the 9–5 favorite to whip the 22-year-old upstart.

In a stunning upset, Vince Foster flattened Tony Pellone in 44 seconds of the seventh round. Tony was down for a four count in the third round, a no count in the fourth and finally twice in the fatal seventh. Long right hands followed by crunching left hooks to the body did Tony in. He took the full ten count. The fans were stunned, never having seen Tony down before. The *New York News* Saturday Edition had a large photo of Foster standing over a downed Pellone with the words, "Tough Tony Hardened—in Starch." It was a sensational win, very impressive. This kid had the old-timers of the era buzzing. He looked like the real article. One could see real greatness in this solid socking brawler. Only thing was, there was a flaw; he was too good to be true. The fans would find out soon enough.

The Garden promoters couldn't have been happier. With Foster's great KO win over Pellone and Charley's fine win over Rocky Castellani, what better fight could they come up with than Foster vs. Fusari? A real punchers' battle. They went for it. The winner of this fight would be pitted against the "Dead End Kid" Rocky Graziano, outdoors. The New York State Athletic Commission was getting ready to reinstate Graziano after a three-year suspension. The Foster-Fusari winner would welcome back Rock-a-Bye Rocky in a city ballpark. Lots of great action ahead for the fans. Foster was made the favorite over Charley, probably because they were using Tony Pellone as a yardstick. Fusari had lost to Pellone. Foster had run over Pellone like a steamroller for a sensational kayo win over the Greenwich Village tough guy. The fight was set for May 13, 1945.

Before the first-round bell had faded away, Foster was on the attack. He landed the same crunching and bruising left hooks to Fusari's body that had set up Pellone. They only shook Charley. Foster came rushing in to deliver more of the same and was caught with the best of Fusari. A smashing right hand, flush on his jaw. It dropped the westerner for the first of three trips to the canvas, and Fusari's greatest win. Fusari had won a ballpark fight with the homecoming Rock.

For Foster it was his last fight. A bit over two months after his kayo defeat, he was killed in a car crash. His car, traveling at a very high rate of speed, smashed into the rear of a trailer truck. He and a woman companion perished. His manager, Jack Hurley, who had piloted many fighters including Billy Petrolle, the Fargo Express, explained to reporters that this kid Foster was unmanageable. A wild unruly rebel with an unpredictable temperament. Wine, women, partying and speed were his forte. So on that lonely Pipestone, Minnesota, road, this mixed-up kid threw his life away and destroyed what looked like to many, despite the Fusari loss, a great talent as a fighter that could have made him very rich and famous. What a tremendous waste. It was all at his fingertips for the taking. But playing the part of the fool was more important. He was one month away from his 22nd birthday.

Fusari was on top of the world. He would now face the former middleweight champion of the world, the very popular Rocky Graziano. Their fight would be set for mid–September 1949 in New York's Polo Grounds. Rocky would be the favorite because of his huge punching ability. The Rock-a-Bye Baby would also have a pull in the weights of 12 pounds. Those close to the sport gave Fusari a good chance of pulling the upset. Charley, too, was a good puncher; he was also very durable, never having been knocked out before. He also had developed into a fine boxer. These assets, especially the boxing ability, could bring home the victory for Charley. There was a lot of anticipation before the fight. New Yorkers had missed their beloved "Rocky." He hadn't appeared in that city for three years. They were anxious to get Rocky back a winner.

Charley set up camp at the old "Madame Bey" training camp at Summit, New Jersey, now known as Ehsans. It was one of the most famous training camps in boxing history. All the greats trained there at one time or another. Some friends and I made our way to the site to watch Charley work out. Fusari looked very good in a brisk sparring session with Johnny "Red" DeFazio. After his workout, Charley hit the shower. Most of the fans waited for him outside, hoping to talk to him and maybe get a snapshot of their favorite fighter. Charley came out and graciously talked and shook hands with his fans. I was able to wish him good luck against Graziano with a handshake. Charley also stood still for the cameras before his team whisked him off. We were able to get two snaps of Charley, which I still have to this day. He appeared more than ready and confident for the biggest fight of his life.

Graziano came into the ring a fit 159½ pounds. Fusari scaled 147½. These two warriors put on a great fight, with Rocky throwing his usual bombs and pursuing the Irvington Blond. Charley kept sticking out his jab and making Rocky miss. Fusari mixed it up with straight jarring rights that stung Rocky more than once. They would often engage in spirited exchanges, in some of which Charley came out on top. Fusari had to be very careful in these exchanges. Slugging it out with Rocky was like handling a rattler. One mistake and you're out. Going into the ninth round, Fusari was doing so well he took all-out liberties with Rocky and won the round big. Going into the tenth and last round,

Fusari was ahead on all scorecards. Rocky was swinging like a gate, huge haymakers. Fusari was punching back while slipping the bombs. Rocky had become totally desperate and came on in maniacal charges. One bomb finally caught Charley on the chin, driving him against the ropes. Charley was in trouble. Rocky battered Charley along the ropes, and Fusari slid to the canvas. Charley took nine and got up wobbly. Graziano was on him like a cat slinging rights and lefts into his helpless foe until the referee stopped the deadly onslaught with less than a minute left to the final bell. Fusari could have played it safe, and he would have walked away with the decision. But that just wouldn't be Charley Fusari. He was a fighter first and always.

In the next eight months, Charley would fight in Madison Square Garden three times. Terry Young was badly beaten into an eighth-round stoppage. Jimmy Flood was thrashed in ten rounds. Fusari romped. He then fought Paddy Young in a brutal ten-rounder won by Young by *one point*, a slam-bang battle that most observers thought Charley won, including your writer. Ironically it was the third Garden main bout that Charley lost by split decision. Give the man a break, please.

The break, if anyone can call it that, was a shot at the championship of the world. A chance at the title is the pinnacle of every fighter's dreams. The goal that only so few achieve. The pot of gold at rainbow's end. Only for Charley it was never sugar and honey. The only sugar in this deal was "Sugar" Ray Robinson, the welterweight champ. He offered to defend his title against Charley at Roosevelt Stadium in Jersey City. Charley was a top contender, and Robby figured the challengers backyard would be the right place. This was a fight Charley couldn't win. He and his team knew only a miracle could bring Charley home a winner. He would be up against the greatest fighter to ever lace on a glove. Robby would enter the ring with only one loss in over 100 fights. Robinson could box, punch and had an iron chin. Some people believed Charley's great right hand was his only hope. If they checked, Robby had fought the best punchers in three divisions, lightweight, welter and middleweight, and no one came near kayoing him.

Robinson was having a difficult time making the 147-pound limit. He had defended his title four times in three years. Rules called for two defenses a year. It wasn't Robinson's fault he was behind in title bouts. Some of the contenders turned down offers to fight for the championship. They knew they couldn't win. A situation unheard of in boxing history. That's how good Robby was. Robby didn't mind this turn of events because making 147 was getting to be almost impossible for him. He kept busy fighting middleweights. He'd like to hold on to the welterweight title until he could get a middleweight champ into the ring with him. He had to make a welterweight defense in 1950 or run the risk of getting stripped by the commission. Fusari was offered the bout, and he took it. Charley would fight an army tank; he believed in himself. One had to feel sorry for Fusari; he had fought long and hard to get a title shot, only to get his chance at a *super* champ. Charley would be a huge, huge underdog.

At the weigh-in, Charley looked to be in great shape. Robby looked drawn and gaunt from hours of steam-room time and crash dieting. This, some Fusari supporters were wishful in their thinking, might be the key for a Fusari win. Robinson would be weak and not at his best, especially in the later rounds.

In August of 1950 Sugar Ray Robinson took on Charley Fusari in that Jersey City ring, the undisputed title up for grabs. The fight was a *sparring* session. Robinson retained his title with a 15-round decision. The referee Paul Cavalier had it 13–1–1, Robinson. At that time, New Jersey used the referee as lone judge. He and only he decided the winner. Robby simply outclassed Fusari, never setting down on his punches; it was a boxing clinic. Robinson must have decided not to go to war with the youngster. He was so weak from making weight, it would be easier to just box smoothly to an easy decision. There was some talk after the fight that Charley midway through the bout told his corner he was ready to "go for broke." Cooler heads told him if the champ wants to box, box. The loss certainly didn't hurt Fusari. Nobody beats Sugar Ray, yet Charley could say he went the 15-round route with the best.

In February of 1951, Robinson won the middleweight championship. That left his welterweight title vacant. The National Boxing Association (NBA) set up a match between Charley Fusari vs. Johnny Bratton for their version of the title. The New York Commission had Kid Gavilan as their title holder. Fusari went to Chicago to fight Bratton in Johnny's hometown. He did himself proud. In a grueling 15-round *war*, Charley fought one of the best fights of his career. Although dropped twice in the contest, Charley came back like a man possessed, meeting Bratton toe to toe in a torrid bout. Bratton, a slick boxer-puncher, was a fighter who had ups and downs in his career, but when he was on, he was *on*. Charley met him on his on night, and what a brawl it was. TV viewers across the country disagreed with the split decision Bratton received. I believe if the fight was held in New York City, Fusari would have won the title.

Kid Gavilan would defeat Bratton to claim the full title. Fusari went on to meet the up-and-coming Gil Turner, a real whirlwind hard puncher who was undefeated.

It was another barnburner with both boys going all out. Fusari was floored in the 11th round for the count. Turner was quoted as saying, "I said a prayer so that guy wouldn't beat the count. I had enough of him for one evening."

Charley took time off and returned to the ring half a year later. He was lucky to gain the decision over Jimmy Champagne, a local club fighter. Charley thought the layoff was responsible for his poor showing and took a rematch three weeks later. Charley had nothing left and was easily out pointed. Fusari was smart enough to see this and retired for good. No comebacks as most fighters do. Charley was 27½ years old.

Insiders in the know could see why Charley's skills had eroded so soon. Charley always fought hard. His fights from the Graziano bout to the Gil Turner fight was a two-year period in which Fusari left all he had in the ring. What more can any fight fan ask of a fighter?

My memorial to Charley is this story—my way of paying him for my being able to reminisce, to jog one's memory back in time into a "twilight zone" of boxing, to a decade when boxing was king.

One can turn off the television set. Ignore that book with its stale story. Relax in an easy chair, close one's eyes and click one's mind back to the *posters*, for a full evening of enjoyment. Immediately the grand years of 1944 through 1947 focus into play. The undefeated Fusari years dance across the scene and bring with them the golden age of New Jersey boxing. The fistic career of Charley Fusari, the Blond Bomber, aka "The Irvington Milkman," the "Golden Boy" of the times. A time of *many* fight clubs, offering fights to a legion of fighters, good ones, who battled it out for recognition. The preliminary boxers who fought on the under-cards were as important and adored by the fans as the main-eventers. One could pick out the future stars among them and follow their careers as they worked their way up the pugilistic ladder. What a great time it was for fight fans. A time which sadly will never be seen again. The sports pages of your local newspapers were full of boxing news and file photos of the favorites of the time in their fighting poses. A fan was able to make a scrapbook of his heroes. That would be impossible in recent times; most sports pages are barren of boxing news.

With so little fight news covered by the media, I am often compelled to click on the posters to my favorite time, when always the top name was in red and always the name on top was Fusari. Along with fans of Charley's that are still around, we believe the name Fusari was always in red his entire career because he was our favorite, win, lose or draw.

Joe Louis's "Exhibitions":
Joe Cheshul and
Henry "Snow" Flakes

Joe Louis, living legend, the heavyweight champion of the world, the beloved Brown Bomber, announced his retirement. With his 11th-round knockout and second win over his challenger and antagonist, Jersey Joe Walcott, Louis knew his come-from-behind kayo of the Camden Cutie was stretching it very thin.

Their first fight was very controversial. Many, in fact the majority, thought Walcott had garnered the decision and the title. In their two fights Walcott had dropped the Bomber *three times*. Louis made up his mind, it was time to go. Immediately after the ten count was completed over Walcott, Louis announced his intentions to public and press. "To my mother, this is for her. This was my last fight." The date was June 25, 1948. Site, Yankee Stadium, New York, New York. His official retirement would come in letter form to the respective boxing commissions on March 1, 1949.

This opened the throne room doors for the first time in over 11 years to mortal heavyweights. With the invincible one gone, a challenger now had a chance to win that crown which Louis had defended a record-breaking 25 times. He took on anyone who had a claim to a title match. Twenty-two challengers were knocked senseless. Only three lasted the distance of 15 rounds. Louis dodged no one. It's a record that will never be broken.

The champ's decision to vacate set off a frenzy of competitive fights between the best "*Young Lions*" of the day. There were many. Sluggers, boxers, maulers, they were competent and very ambitious. All ready to win the big title. The NBA (National Boxing Association) along with

Joe Louis and his endorsement agreed that Ezzard Charles, the number-one contender, would face Jersey Joe Walcott for the vacant crown. The Young Lions were contending to get the winner of this match, the thinking being that it would be much easier to win over a *small* Ezzard Charles or an *old* Walcott than tackling the great Brown Bomber even at his advanced age.

It is this writer's pleasure to name the Young Lions, for they fought their hearts out. Sadly, over time most have been forgotten. Yet their families and friends and some old-timers will get a lift to know they haven't been entirely forgotten.

From Europe came Gino Bounvino, an Italian; Harry Berntsen, from Norway; and Cesar Brion of the Argentine. Two New Jersey boys: Joe Cheshul of Bayonne and Willis "Red" Applegate of Montclair. New York's Roland La Starza, Carmine Vingo, and Henry "Snow" Flakes. One Canadian was in the mix, Don Mogard. Gene Gosney was a cowboy from Texas by way of Oklahoma. Vern Mitchell of Detroit and Art Swiden from Pittsburgh. From the west was Rex Layne of Utah; Bernie Reynolds was from Fairfield, Connecticut. And Jackie Cranford from Washington, D.C. And let's not forget a fellow from Brockton, Massachusetts, Rocky Marciano. It was fun seeing the best of the bunch rise to the top. Something like before milk was homogenized. The cream settled to the top of the bottle. And so it was with the Young Lions. Marciano, La Starza, Rex Layne, Cesar Brion, and Henry "Snow" Flakes all became top-ten contenders, Joe Cheshul in a fringe position. My favorites were Marciano, Flakes and Cheshul. The latter two became a mystery to this very young fan at the time. More on that later.

Marciano fought seven of the other 15 lions. He knocked out four and decisioned three. Jerseyite Willis "Red" Applegate, Don Mogard and Roland La Starza were three of the only five men to take Rocky to the scorecards. That's how tough this group was. Applegate can also be remembered as the first man to take Blackjack Billy Fox to a decision. He also pulled the upset, gaining the nod.

Gino Bounvino and Carmine Vingo along with Rex Layne had the audacity and cojones to meet Marciano head on. Talk about brave young men. Here is where boxing people often overlook Rocky's power. Bounvino met Rocky twice in all-out wars and was kayoed in the tenth and final round in the first fight. In the return Gino was blasted out in six.

97

Gino was never the same after those Rocky fights. Carmine Vingo, a fine prospect, met Rocky at Madison Square Garden in a battle that Rocky always claimed to be the toughest of his career. Vingo was blasted to the canvas in the sixth round of a rousing slugfest. Each man staggered time and again. Vingo was seriously injured and had to undergo brain surgery. Needless to say a fine promising career came to a close. Rex Layne would meet Rocky at MSG in a brawl and was brutally kayoed. Layne was never the same fighter after this loss. Marciano did it time and again. When he was through with an opponent, that fighter's career was practically over, especially the ones that slugged it out with the Rock. Gene Gosney, the very tough cowboy, made a name for himself with barnburners against Gino Bounvino and Roland La Starza and a much talked about sparring session with Marciano in a New York City gym. These two human bulls met head on in a slugfest. Onlookers couldn't believe the savagery. Those fortunate enough to be there to witness the "workout" gave Rocky the nod.

Harry Berntsen, the lad from Norway, was included in with the Young Lions because of his fan-popular blood-and-guts style that made him a favorite in the New York City clubs. He fought the best and had a spotty record because of it. He was a huge test for any of the lions. While working on the docks as a stevedore between fights, he was killed in a work-related accident.

One of the lions was a mystery to me as mentioned earlier. Henry "Snow" Flakes from Buffalo, New York, never competed against any of the others. That was the mystery. His last fight only a month before Joe Louis announced his retirement was a ten-round decision over world-rated crafty Lee Oma, his second over Lee in ten days, the first fight also being a ten round win. That was in June 1948, six months into the year, and Flakes had already fought ten main events. He was very active. The two Oma wins, one at MSG, followed two huge victories over the top-ranked dangerous Pat Comiskey of Paterson, New Jersey, whom Flakes had decisioned at Akron, Ohio. Comiskey and his manager Bill Daly, who were coasting along to a title match, were stunned. This young battler fought Pat punch for punch, trading all the way with the power-punching Jersey Irishman and gaining a popular decision. Bill Daly demanded a return match immediately but on Comiskey's turf. That would be in the Newark Armory in two weeks; Daly figured a Comiskey win just days after his defeat would prove the first fight to be a fluke. The expected win would keep Pat's lofty position in the world ratings secure and keep alive his title hopes.

Flakes was no stranger to the Newark, New Jersey, fans. They and the writer had seen him just ten months before fighting a six-round prelim to the Pat Comiskey–Joe Muscato fight. Muscato was from Buffalo, New York, also, and he brought along his stable mates for some action. They called him Henry "Korn" Flakes that night. Comiskey kayoed Muscato in two rounds. Flakes won his six rounder and impressed. Just months later he would be in the same ring with Comiskey in the main event. How's that for progress? This time it was Henry "Snow" Flakes, and he scored a sensational knockout over Comiskey, putting Pat down for the full count with a blizzard of punches from the "Snowflakes." It was only the second time Comiskey was counted out in a lengthy career. His only other kayo conqueror was the dynamic punching former heavyweight champion Max Baer. What an accomplishment for this young Buffalo Bopper. He engaged Comiskey from the first bell in a bruising brawl. Both men were banged up bad. They were throwing knockout punches all the way. Two smashing rights drove Comiskey into the ropes badly hurt. Another right and Pat clinched Flakes; then Flakes drove four more sledgehammer rights to Pat's jaw, felling him like an ox to one knee. Comiskey was counted out in that position—a fifth-round kayo win for the youngster from Buffalo. Although he had won a decision the first time they met, Flakes was an 18–5 underdog going in this time.

Henry "Snow" Flakes was indeed a mystery. Boxing writers hustled around trying to find background information on him. Some newspapers couldn't even get his name right. They wrote him up as Henry "Snowflakes" Blake. It was discovered Flakes never fought as an amateur. He was learning on the job since his pro debut. In 1947 Flakes fought 17 times, winning 16, losing only one but scoring ten kayos with no soft touches.

From his performance with Comiskey alone, this writer believed Flakes could "get it on" with Walcott and Charles, or even the Rock. This 21-year-old showed it all against Comiskey. He could box, punch, and take a punch. He showed courage and a great will to win. Flakes followed with the two wins over Lee Oma and disappeared. There was no explanation in metropolitan newspapers. The boxing commissions must have known, but to the regular fight fan this man came out of nowhere and then was gone. Your writer believes managerial problems put Flakes on the shelf, or maybe a detached retina ended his career as happened much too often in those days. Months passed and no Flakes fights. It was hard to believe a fighter in his position would give up a career that was rolling into high gear. In only 18 months of fisticuffing Flakes established himself as a top-ten contender. He packed in 27 fights, losing only two. He had everything going for him. His last fight against Lee Oma at Madison Square Garden showed he was improving in every outing. He actually outboxed the clever Oma in the final rounds. Flakes was a definite front-runner in the scramble for the heavyweight "bauble."

Rumor had it that he got in trouble with the law in his hometown and was jailed, although nothing was ever seen in print by the writer. In time Flakes was forgotten.

Years later, mystery solved. While watching the History Channel on the topic of U.S. prisons, up popped a shot of Henry Flakes and Sing Sing Prison. He was executed there for killing a liquor store proprietor during a holdup.

So it was—on the brink of stardom. His potential unlimited, he threw it all away. What demon possessed him? He certainly didn't need the money at the time of the shooting, or so it appeared. He was averaging two main events a month and winning.

Sad, tragic, there are no words for it. Henry "Snow" Flakes, instead of leaving a great boxing legacy, all he had left was a question for trivia fans. Who was the only heavyweight top-ten contender to die in the electric chair? A very little-known fact for boxing buffs. What a waste. The guy had talent. Championship timber. As Larry Merchant would say, "Boxing, the theater of the unexpected."

Joe Louis and his team went on to an exhibition tour of South America almost immediately after his announced retirement. Joe was broke. He never really knew how to handle money, and most of his "boxing friends," to put it mildly, took advantage of him. Joe believed he was a very good golfer. He loved to play, but Joe had golf "friends" also. These golf buddies were nothing more than "sharks"; they'd let Joe win a few for small stakes. When they got Joe pumped up, Joe would ask the stakes to be raised. Then the sharks would lay it on him. Joe lost untold thousands on the golf links. Louis was also an easy mark for any sad story. The hangers-on and the leeches bled Joe dry.

The South American tour was a washout. The exhibitions consisted of four three-minute rounds with headgear and heavy training gloves worn by both men. The fans attending demanded more action. They started staying away.

The Louis team had to rethink this situation. They were used to the big money. They decided to put on ten-round no-decision exhibitions minus headgear, and ten-ounce gloves would be used. The extra two ounces would make it possible that the bouts could be called exhibitions. Today's heavyweight bouts are fought with the ten ounce gloves, the commissions over the years adding the ounces to show their attempt at reducing fatalities. So the Louis exhibitions were fought with all the regulations we have in real fights today. Except if the fight went the distance, it would be no decision. The Louis team figured the ND 10 would be an insurance policy in case an opponent might outpoint Joe. The only way Louis could lose is he would have to be knocked out, which was very unlikely because Louis's only threat would be the title holder himself, Ezzard Charles, who became champ after Joe retired.

The Louis team decided they would pick solid well-known opposition to face Joe. He could fight once a week. He could stay in shape that way, limit the training and keep a steady cash flow coming in. He also would be shaping himself up for that title shot at Ezzard, which he and his handlers denied they wanted. Yet it was their goal all along.

Louis had no choice. He owed the IRS. Johnny Shkor, the huge Polish-American from Boston, was the first on the Louis list of these ten-round, no-decision exhibitions. Shkor was a tough, durable fighter who fought the best around. Louis dropped Johnny three times and trounced him for the entire ten rounds. It was a real fight. Louis was trying to kayo Shkor. The exhibition tag was so much baloney, and everyone knew it. Only days later it would be Joe Cheshul, a young up-and-coming prospect from Bayonne, New Jersey; the "exhibition" would be held at the Newark Armory.

Joe Cheshul, one of our "Young Lions," was chosen because he was well known in the New York and Jersey areas. Not yet a household name, but the potential was there for him to obtain the position of top contender. He was a very good boxer who moved well for a heavyweight. He was called a young "rookie" by boxing writers of the day.

Going into the "exhibition" with Louis, Cheshul had been boxing pro for three and a half years. Although not a power puncher, he had a fine crisp right hand along with his above-average boxing ability. Cheshul had advanced well under the guidance of his manager, Al Thoma, and had recently scored six wins over worthy competition, thereby earning the Louis bout. His first main event was a ten-round win over the Italian entry Renato Tontini at Elizabeth. Joe won easily. His next opponent was Fidel Arciniega, Spain's entry to the heavyweight ranks. Fidel was stopped in six rounds. With each win Al Thoma would step up the talent of the opponent. Cheshul was then matched with Willis "Red" Applegate, another Young Lion, but Red pulled out sick. He was replaced by Leo Matriccini, a tough Baltimore heavy who had recently held Applegate to a draw. In a rousing fight, Cheshul outpointed the heavier Matriccini. Art Swiden was selected next for Cheshul. Joe was a dandy that night, winning every round.

Cheshul's first main event at Madison Square Garden was a ten-round decision over the rough tough Gene Gosney, another Young Lion. Joe followed up this fine win with a victory over Vern Mitchell, also a lion and highly touted. Cheshul turned the tables on Mitchell who a month earlier had decisioned him. Sweet revenge for the young prospect. Joe was improving with each fight. When the Louis "exhibition" was offered, Manager Thoma accepted. He knew if Cheshul looked good in the bout with the aging Bomber, Cheshul would be in line for some lucrative fights.

Joe Louis and Joe Cheshul got it on at the Newark, New Jersey, Armory on November 22, 1949. Five thousand five hundred fans turned out, and the gate was $19,200 gross. Louis scaled 228½ pounds and Cheshul came in at 185. Louis was 36 years old, Cheshul 25. Cheshul gave up 43½ pounds and tons of experience to the former champion. The crowd was buzzing as the principals entered the ring. It was a happy crowd. Many people such as myself had gotten the opportunity to see the living legend Joe Louis in the flesh. Never mind he was retired and no longer held the title. It didn't matter. Everyone liked Louis; he was a very popular champion and a credit to boxing. The crowd, I believe, wanted to see both men do well. Cheshul was well liked in Jersey rings, and a large Bayonne contingent was in attendance. Heavy betting was going on, mostly on how many rounds it would take Louis to kayo the upstart, or if he could last the full ten.

Louis came out in the first round as he always did, shuffling straight in wearing those royal purple trunks. Cheshul looked like he was in awe of the great one. And who could blame him? Louis's ramrod left jab was on display. It was still as good as I saw it at his training camp at Pompton Lakes before the second Walcott fight. To this day, some 57 years after Louis-Cheshul, I still believe Louis had the greatest left jab of any heavyweight that ever lived. His jab was a deadly weapon. He could bust up an opponent and even floor some with that punch. Other heavyweights with powerful jabs I've seen over the years were Lee Savold; it is said he broke more noses, including Billy Conn's, than any other fighter. Paterson, New Jersey, heavy Pat Comiskey had a great jab, learning from stable mate Savold. Sonny Liston had a very damaging jab and relied on it constantly. But Joe Louis was tops in the jab department. His was the red ramrod of reality.

Cheshul had to get away from that jab or he wouldn't go far. He settled down in the second round and was using his own jab against the Bomber. Louis kept throwing the jab with an occasional right hand, always pressing for a chance to score the coup de grâce. As the rounds slipped by, the atmosphere in the huge drill shed was filled with drama. Could the young man last the limit? Louis kept coming after Cheshul who circled and backed away from Louis's power. After each round's end there was applause for Cheshul. As they approached the midpoint of the fight, Cheshul began taking liberties and getting aggressive. A smashing right hand to the jaw dropped the youngster. He got up at nine. His left eye was cut and bleeding. Although he tried, Louis could not catch the elusive Cheshul with his big punch again. Cheshul finished the full ten rounds to the delight of his fans and himself. It was an interesting, good fight; the fans enjoyed it. Your writer thought Cheshul did himself proud. Yet if you were to read the *New York News* write-up the next day, it was hard to believe the writer of that article was indeed at the fight. He wrote it cut and dry as if Cheshul did nothing.

The truth of the matter was this: here was a young fighter with only 25 fights on his resume giving over 43 pounds to an all-time great puncher, climbing off the floor with a cut eye (many fighters would have bailed out at that point) and finishing the full ten rounds. Louis left the ring with a "mouse" under his left eye, proving Cheshul had a pretty good left jab himself. I recall leaving the Armory and thinking another year and Joe Cheshul would be right up there with the top ten. Some people would say Louis was washed up. He was too old to get Cheshul out of there. Nonsense. Louis at age 36 could still beat all the heavyweights but one, the then champ. As the months would pass, that fact proved true. Cheshul completed ten rounds because of his slick boxing and sheer gameness.

My thinking that Joe Cheshul would make the top ten was dashed only four months after his fine showing against Joe Louis. Cheshul earned an MSG match against another fine prospect, the heavy-punching Joe Lindsay. Cheshul was stopped, the first time in his career. He retired from boxing. Many thought it was premature of Joe to hang them up. He had a lot of talent and was still young and improving. Cheshul made his decision and stuck with it. He never made a comeback. Another strange happening in boxing.

The Cheshul-Lindsay fight was the semifinal to the battle between undefeated Rocky Marciano and Roland La Starza, two Young Lions duking it out for big-time recognition. Rocky squeaked by in a very close fight, winning by three points. The lone knockdown he scored made the difference. The closeness of the fight kept La Starza in the mix along with the Rock for a title bout. Joe Cheshul, Henry "Snow" Flakes and Harry Berntsen left the Young Lions club. Some of the others were battle worn from fighting with each other.

Next up was Johnny Flynn, the site Kansas City. Flynn was a top-ten heavy who fought the best in the division. He was a respected opponent for any heavyweight. Flynn was durable and was able to stay the limit with the Bomber despite being dropped two times.

West Coast heavyweight Pat Valentino was next. It was scheduled for Chicago. Valentino had recently fought for the Heavyweight Championship of the World against champion Ezzard Charles. In a torrid rip-roaring fight, Charles was able to flatten Valentino for the full ten count in the eighth round. Joe Louis could see that these ten-round, no-decision exhibitions weren't bringing in the cash as first predicted.

They had to drop that exhibition tag; the name alone was defined by boxing fans as boring, no matter how it was presented. Even though

Louis was very aggressive, making the exhibitions real, trying for the kayo win, the fans knew the result would go into the record books an EXND 10. Many if not all the exhibitions would never get listed in the records of the fighters. Example: check Joe Cheshul's record. He never got the credit for having faced the great Brown Bomber and extending him the full ten rounds. It's as if the fight never happened. You would have to take his word that he indeed fought Joe Louis or track down a record book that did record the result.

Louis had to honor his contract that called for three more such contests. He would finish them up and start his official comeback, as he should have done in the first place. Louis decided to prove to the fans that he was just as good as or better than Ezzard Charles. He would prove it by kayoing Pat Valentino faster then Ezzard did while defending his title against the tough brawler. Louis would do it in his so-called exhibition bout with the Italian-American contender, thereby also proving unwittingly that these exhibitions were *real* fights right from the beginning.

Louis pounded Valentino throughout the first seven rounds and flattened him for the ten count late in the eighth round. Valentino was never in the fight. He took a shellacking. Against Charles in their title bout, Valentino fought a barnburner with Ez, going toe to toe in an even fight till the eighth. Joe Louis had matched the champion on their conquests of Valentino. Louis was more impressive, but had Charles softened up Valentino for Louis to slaughter?

Next up would be Al Hoosman at Oakland, California. Hoosman was a 6'6" well-built heavyweight who fought so many bouts in Europe he became a huge favorite over there. They even wrote a book about him. Joe Louis tore the giant up and knocked him cold in the fifth round. Another fine KO that would not enhance Louis's knockout record. Reason—it was an "exhibition."

The situation was getting ridiculous. Bernie Reynolds, a Young Lion, decided to pull out of a scheduled exhibition with Louis that was penciled in for Detroit. He claimed an injury. Nick Londos, the promoter, had Lee Oma under contract, and it was decided to use Oma, the "Clown Prince of Sock," to replace Reynolds. When Tex Sullivan, Oma's manager, heard of it he hit the roof. Sullivan was a Damon Runyon–type character who was the epitome of the Hollywood boxing manager. Tex bellowed, and we quote, "These aren't exhibitions; they're real wars. Look what happened to Valentino. Louis isn't planning a comeback. He's already come back. *We're* not afraid of Louis, but if it's going to be a real fight, let's advertise it that way. Then we *both* can make some money." End of quote. Finally some good sound sense was offered and accepted by the Louis team. Only Oma didn't get the Louis fight. They dumped the remaining exhibitions and went right for the throat—Ezzard's throat—and the shot at his title which they were after from the start.

The reader should know that there was nothing wrong or shady about the exhibitions, nor did Louis do anything wrong. Louis was honorable and would never hurt boxing. Louis was only doing what his "brain trust" had concocted for him. The Bomber tried to please the fans by going for the kayo to enhance the fights and lift the gate receipts, and also to fight himself into shape for the Ezzard Charles match which they knew was waiting ahead.

Looking back, it wasn't fair to Johnny Shkor, Joe Cheshul, Johnny Flynn, Pat Valentino, or Al Hoosman. Their hard-fought battles against the great Joe Louis are not in the majority of record books. Louis's record off the Internet is minus their names. It's also a loss of five wins, two by kayo, for Jolting Joe.

On September 27, 1950, Joe Louis would challenge the man who succeeded him as champion of the heavyweights, Ezzard Charles. No bogus tag on this fight, it was for all the marbles. Charles was NBA champion. Champ in all states but New York. They would recognize the winner as true world champion. Louis came in at 218. Ezzard won the unanimous decision with lopsided scores. Louis relied on his left jab the entire fight; Ezz claimed that's all Louis had left. Photos of the two combatants after the fight show just what that Louis left jab could do. Ezzard's eyes and face were badly swollen, even though he won wide. Joe's face was also a mess. Ezz was in his prime. Joe was not.

Joe Louis would fight eight more times, winning all eight, five by decision three by kayo. He then fought the undefeated Rocky Marciano in Madison Square Garden. It would be his last fight. Rocky would knock Louis out of the ring onto the apron. Referee Ruby Goldstine didn't have the heart to count the great former champion out and showed his respect for the Bomber by not doing so. He called a halt after that second knockdown. Even Rocky was not proud or happy with himself after his big win. Everybody liked Joe Louis. Rocky was in his prime; Louis was not. Both fighters had swollen faces, again proving the power in Joe's left hand. It served him well against Charles and Marciano. It was 99 percent of Joe's arsenal in those two fights. One has to think what the results would be if Louis also was in his prime with all his weapons intact. That's a question for the ages.

The Russian Lion
and the Philly Fox

In the early part of his career, nothing came easy for Gus Lesnevich. In boxing Gus was known as the honest workman, a good puncher, a fair boxer who was gifted with courage beyond belief. His main drawback was he cut easily. Only brave Chuck Wepner bled more than Lesnevich.

In his favor was his friendship with Joe Vella, who became his manager. It was Vella who got Gus started in the amateurs. Lesnivich and Vella were born on the same street in Cliffside Park, New Jersey. They would remain friends for life.

When Gus first started in boxing as a pro, he fought many bloody, grueling wars for chump change because that's what fighters were paid in those years following the Great Depression. A fighter had to fight often and hard to make a living and provide for his family. Gus's best friend could attest to that, he being James J. Braddock of "Cinderella Man" fame. Gus and Braddock were also lifetime buddies, and both were a credit to boxing. They were alike—Depression fighters. It made them extra tough and mean. It's simple; they were *hungry*. Hard times make extra hard fighters.

Gus fought his way through the prelim bouts, blood spattered all the way. There were many good fighters around the New York–New Jersey club circuit, so Gus learned his trade well. Some of the tough hombres he clashed with were Jackie Aldare, John Anderson and two slugfests at Laurel Garden with Frankie Caris. He then moved on to California, fighting the best on that coast; then Down Under, Gus made a name for himself with three big wins in Australia, losing only to Ron Richards, one of Australia's very best.

On Gus's return to the states, Joe Louis was prepping at Pompton Lakes, New Jersey, for a title bout with Tony Galento, the Orange, New Jersey, Bad Boy. Louis had a young fighter whom he thought so much of that he called him his protégé. The kid's name was Dave Clark; he had a sparkling record, and Louis believed Clark would one day become champion. When Louis opened camp at Pompton, he brought along his protégé as a sparring partner. Louis thought, what could possibly be a better way to introduce my charge to East Coast fans than have him knock off a top contender like Gus Lesnevich, a Jersey fighter? He, Louis, was of course a huge favorite to stop Galento, and Joe figured Clark would take out Lesnevich. Louis believed they would both go back to Detroit winners, leaving the Jersey boys in the resin.

They would soon find out just how tough these Garden State battlers were. Clark was installed a 4–1 favorite. The bell rang for Lesnevich vs. Clark, with Joe Louis in his young colleague's corner. It was all over in 1:28 seconds of the very first round. Gus landed a bomb on the highly publicized prospect's jaw. Gus earned himself a shot at Billy Conn's light heavyweight title at MSG. Clark would return home a knockout loser, and Joe Louis had to climb off the canvas to retain his crown. That's boxing. A puncher always has a chance.

Lesnevich met Billy Conn, the Pittsburgh Kid, but lost the decision in a spirited fight. Gus then gave Dave Clark a return bout. Dave's people demanded it. They claimed the first fight was a fluke. They still couldn't believe the stunning knockout he suffered at Gus's hands. Clark did better the second time around. He lost again, but by decision. Gus got another shot at Conn but again lost a 15-round decision. Scribes called Gus "the Patient Plodder."

Billy Conn relinquished his light heavyweight title. The National Boxing Association recognized the winner of the Anton Christoforidis–Gus Lesnevich fight as their champion. Gus won the 15-round decision over the tough Greek champion. Gus's first defense would be against Tami Mauriello, a sensational young New York City product. Gus got the 15-round split decision and added the New York Commission's blessing as undisputed Light Heavyweight Champion of the World. He gave Tami a rematch and won on all cards in another great fight with the New Yorker. The Second World War started three weeks later. Gus would take two fights against top-rated heavyweights Bob Pastor and Jimmy

Bivins. He lost by decision to both. Lesnevich joined the U.S. Coast Guard in 1942 and spent all his time teaching the Guardsmen how to box and defend themselves. Three and a half years in the service was a huge loss of prime years to the fighter. Gus did it without complaints and received an honorable discharge in 1945. Lesnevich was pushing 31 and hadn't fought in almost four years. He never really made big money before the war, so now was his time before it ran out.

His first fight back would be against a young Woodburn, Oregon, fighter who was being touted as a world beater, Joe Kahut. The fight would take place at Portland, Oregon, and a full house was expected to see the local young farmer trounce the champion. This would be a non-title ten-rounder. No soft pickings for Gus. Even though his friend and manager Joe Vella was still in the Army, Gus took this dangerous fight. He needed the money, and he could make it with Kahut. Gus had his faithful trainer Allie Rigeway with him. Nat Fleischer, the *Ring* magazine editor, would referee. Gus explained later, "I was real nervous, more so than when I was an amateur. It was like starting all over at thirty-one."

Kahut didn't last a full round. Gus pulled another Dave Clark kayo. The 22-year-old sensation was never in the fight.

It was now time to defend the title which the war put in mothballs for four years. Time for Gus to earn some real money. He was offered a huge purse to fight Freddy Mills, the British champion, in London. No one could blame Gus for sidestepping his number-one challenger, Ezzard Charles. Mills would be easy money, and Gus deserved the chance to reap. Charles was waxing red hot; to fight him now would be foolish on Gus's part. Joe Vella had to avoid Ezzard in order to get the gold that was so elusive to Gus's grasp before the war. Now was the time for Lesnevich and Vella to make up for 12 years of hard knocks. The next four years and 11 fights were a memorial to the crafty Joe Vella. He not only made Gus more money than all his previous fights combined, but he was also responsible for Gus gaining the Fighter of the Year award for 1947.

Gus won by tenth-round knockout over a very tough Freddy Mills. In a grueling fight, Gus had to fight his heart out to gain the victory. Mills surprised everyone with his all-out challenge. It was a good win for Gus. People took notice. The expected easy win turned out to be a real brawl, and it lifted the Lesnevich image. The bout was held at the

famous Harringay Arena in London. The place was packed, every Englishman in the place rooting for their boy, 26-year-old Mills. Freddy was
a 4–1 underdog, and his fans were thrilled when he gave more than he
took in the first round against the 31-year-old champion. In the second
round Gus found the range and smashed Mills to the canvas four times,
for counts of six, nine, eight and nine. The gritty challenger finished the
round. Had today's three-knockdown rule been in effect, the fight would
have been over. Thank God it wasn't even heard of back then. It would
have ruined a classic. Gus would have won by an easy two-round kayo,
thereby robbing the fans of a blazing fight. Mills came back with a
vengeance in round three and it became a pier-sixer. By the fifth round
Gus's left eye was swollen shut along with a broken nose. Gus was fading
while Mills looked fresher with each round. When the tenth round
started, the Mills fans were sure Freddy was ahead in the scoring, even
with those four second-round knockdowns. It was looking bad for ole
Gus. Mills came out for the tenth like he wanted to finish Lesnevich off,
and they went toe to toe. Out of nowhere Gus landed a smashing right
hand and dropped Mills for a nine count. Mills gained his feet but was
dropped again for nine. The game Englishman made it up once more
but was bowled over again by the wounded Russian Lion. The ref jumped
in to stop it. The battered champion completed a fine night's work. He
had his challenger down a total of seven times in retaining his title.
Lesnevich stock soared.

The Brits took a liking to Lesnevich. He was offered a lucrative
bout with their beloved heavyweight champion Bruce Woodcock. They
met four months after the Mills fight. Gus lost by eighth-round stoppage.
Since winning the light heavy crown, Lesnevich faced four heavyweights,
Jimmy Bivins, Bob Pastor, Lee Oma and Bruce Woodcock. He came up
short in all four. It was time for a light heavyweight title fight.

Crafty Joe Vella again stepped around Ezzard Charles and latched
on to Black Jack Billy Fox, the highly touted kayo artist, as a challenger
in an MSG bout. Not many people complained about the Ezzard snub
because, one, they were curious about the hyped-up "New Brown
Bomber," and two, Ezzard Charles didn't seem to mind being avoided
because he had eyes only for the heavyweight title.

The challenger was called Black Jack Billy from Philly. That was
Billy Fox, the newly heralded Joe Louis. His no-goodnick manager

Blinkey Palermo had the ballyhoo drums working overtime in praise of his well-muscled handsome young dynamo.

Fox turned pro in late 1943 and was fed a diet of mostly inexperienced or worn-out veterans who were ready for the old-age home. Billy could punch pretty well, so he laid these guys out with complete regularity.

Only thing was he had no opposition at all and learned nothing in his first year as a pro. Thirty opponents were counted out, leaving the referee the chore of sending Fox to a neutral corner and completing the ten count. That was the extent of Billy's education up to that point in his career. Thank you, Blinkey Palermo.

Blinkey had huge plans for the slow-witted easygoing youngster. In the second year, Blinkey stepped up Fox's opponents' credibility. Georgie Kochan was probably the first real opponent who might have a chance against the hard-hitting Fox. In a slugfest, Fox put Kochan away in the sixth round. The number of prone bodies in his wake was now about 36 according to what paper you read. Billy crashed the world ratings, and the publicity drums rolled on. Blinkey Palermo was talking title bout with old Gus Lesnevich for that light heavyweight championship. Blinkey had to keep that kayo streak alive. But he also had to get Fox some *known* opponents to push over so a Lesnevich match would be accepted by the boxing public.

He chose a fight with Ossie "Bulldog" Harris, a durable but battle-worn veteran who fought just about everyone, in over 70 fights winning half. He boasted three decision losses to the Bronx Bull Jake LaMotta. Two were by split decision. He also went to the scorecards twice against Sugar Ray Robinson, losing each time. If Jake and Robbie couldn't kayo Harris, it would be a feather in Fox's hat if he could flatten the Bulldog.

Blinkey figured the "Bulldog" was at his career's end. Only the Bulldog didn't know that, and he came to fight. The fight was held in Pittsburgh in April of 1946. The writer was 12 years old at the time, and I too was also taken with Fox and his mighty kayo record. The guy must be the hammer of Thor, thought I. Having a radio with multiple stations, yours truly would each night search the stations trying to find fights broadcast around the country. That night, not even knowing a Fox-Harris match was made, I stumbled on it among other static-ravaged stations. I was happier than a pig in slop. I grabbed a kitchen chair and put it right up to the radio. I heard one hell of a fight that night. Ossie was giving the Brown Fox a real struggle. Rounds were slipping by, and Billy's kayo streak was being threatened. In the seventh and eighth rounds, Billy was trying desperately to bring Harris down, but the durable Bulldog hung in there. That's what made the fight so thrilling— into the ninth and the Bulldog was still there. Fox threw everything he had left at Harris in the tenth and final round in a desperate attempt to kayo the Bulldog. Late in the round he did just that. According to the blow-by-blow commentator, everyone in the arena was on their feet. Fox saved his kayo streak with only seconds left in the last round.

They had to do it again. In the rematch, ironically, the exact same thing happened. Fox had to go all out to kayo Ossie, again in the *last round*. I caught it again on radio out of Philadelphia. Another thriller. Those two fights were the ones I remember Billy Fox for. Blinkey Palermo would give the kid a few more easy kayo victories and claim the body count to be 49 straight KO's. Lesnevich would be number 50 in a title bout. Actually record keepers could only count about 43. It really didn't matter. Kochan and Ossie Harris were the toughest Fox met; the rest had no chance at all. In hindsight they were doing to this kid what was done to Primo Carnera years before. The poor young scrapper really believed his press clippings, and the sad part is he really didn't know how to fight a real contender.

Fox was now ranked about four in the division behind Ezzard Charles, Archie Moore and Lloyd Marshall, three greats. But people wanted to believe that fantastic knockout streak and the coming of the second Joe Louis which the Fox team, including loveable Frankie Carbo, had trumped up.

Fox got the fight with Lesnevich in early 1947. Students of the sport knew Fox was put on his own that night. Blinkey had thrown him out of the nest. He, Fox, would meet a man who could take a punch and also deliver a big punch. Billy was in jeopardy. Swim or sink. Fly or fall. The Brown Fox from Philly, although the favorite, would be welcomed to the world of real professional boxing for the first time by a champion who was an all-around experienced *complete fighter*.

More than 18,000 fans descended on MSG to see Fox continue his line of kayos. Most thought he would do it. Lesnevich was coming off two brutal fights with Mills and Woodcock. He was also 11 years older than the Philly Fox, Gus being 32 and looking his age. Fox was very youthful at just 21. Gus weighed 174½ and Fox 172; it all looked good for Fox. On paper, that is.

From the first-round bell, Gus took charge and never let up. He showed the youngster all the fundamentals of boxing like a ring general plying his trade on a novice. Only in the fourth round did Billy show his vaunted punch. He caught Gus with a beauty that later Lesnevich admitted hurt him bad. Gus clinched and continued with the boxing lesson to end the round. Experience was the key. Lesnevich had it. Fox didn't.

In the tenth round Lesnevich uncorked a lead right hand that floored Fox for an eight count. Getting up very groggy, he was put down again by the rampaging lion. On his way to the canvas, Billy grabbed both the ref and Lesnevich, and all three were down. Referee Johnny Burns stopped the fight. Fox was finished. It was all over at 2:19 of the tenth round. When interviewed by newsmen after the fight, Fox claimed he hurt his right hand early and couldn't do much afterward. A lame excuse. He asked for a rematch with that "old man" and said, "It was just like the first Louis-Schmeling fight." Needless to say, the kid really believed Palermo's hype.

Blinkey Palermo had to squeeze the last drops of blood out of the young Fox. He started another kayo campaign. He'd send Fox in there with a guy who always made Billy look good and yet give a good account of himself. Tough Georgie Kochan was knocked out by Fox for the second time in a good fight. Fox would then take on a very good fighter in Artie Levine, the same Levine that almost took out Sugar Ray Robinson in the Cleveland fight seven months earlier. Fox's advantage was a seven-pound pull in the weight and an opponent who would stand and trade with him. Levine did just that but was finally overpowered in a real blitzkrieg of a battle. That fight was also held at MSG to keep Garden fans' attention on Fox. He followed up with his *third* kayo over Georgie Kochan, also at Madison Square Garden. Blinkey and Carbo would then pull off one of their most infamous shady deeds. They would talk Jake LaMotta, the famous Bronx Bull, the One Man Gang, to take a dive for Fox, thereby gaining Fox a second fight for the title with Lesnevich. The moniker Raging Bull originated in Hollywood. Blinkey and Carbo figured a knockout of LaMotta, a man known to fight fans as unstoppable, would completely sell a second Fox-Lesnevich fight.

LaMotta was obsessed with winning the middleweight championship. He lived to become champion, yet he knew he'd never get a title shot. He simply refused to use any manager of the New York Managers' Guild. He managed himself but used his brother Joey as manager of record. In short LaMotta wouldn't share any of his purses with anyone. This didn't sit well with the hoods in boxing at the time. LaMotta actually disqualified himself out of a title match. When approached by the fixers, LaMotta turned down the money that was offered. He would "go into the tank" on only one condition. They had to promise him a title shot. Which they did. Jake also requested one other thing. He would not be floored by Fox; after all, Jake was proud of the fact that he was never knocked off his feet in his entire career. And he wanted to keep it that way. He had a large ego to satisfy. Jake agreed to take all of Fox's bombs until the referee called a halt. He knew he could do it. Fox would pull no punches.

In the fourth round at MSG, LaMotta stood against the ropes, and Fox took target practice on Jake's head with full fury, delivering an avalanche of punches; the fight was stopped with Jake still on his feet but supposedly defenseless. Some 18 months later Jake got his title shot and made good. Only the rotten hoods made Jake pay $20,000 to one of the champion's handlers for agreeing to the match. Oh yeah, we believe the handler got the money.

Some of the more knowledgeable in the sport figured the LaMotta-Fox fight wasn't on the up and up. But most believed Fox was puncher enough to really stop LaMotta. (Years later, before a Senate investigation committee, Jake admitted the dive.)

A few months after LaMotta, Fox was back at the Garden, again facing Gus Lesnevich for his light heavyweight title. Blinkey and Carbo had completed their skullduggery. The second Fox-Lesnevich fight packed the Garden, the reason being Gus had a great 1947. He had stopped Fox in February of 1947 and then kayoed Melio Bettina, a top heavyweight, in just 59 seconds of the first round, setting a Garden KO record as the fastest main-event kayo. He turned down an offer to fight Joe Louis and went on to defeat his old rival, another top heavyweight, Tami Mauriello, in a slugfest. In a return match with Tami, Gus finally stopped him in seven rounds at the Garden. That was his fourth win over Mauriello.

Gus was red hot, and he just destroyed the Bronx Barkeep. The sell-out crowd expected fireworks. The Fox team told their man, "Go out there and get him into a slugging match—don't let him box you." Fox did what he was told and was blown out of there in 1:58 of the first round, another blazing first-round win for the Russian Lion.

Fox came out slugging, and Gus was happy to oblige. During a furious exchange, a big right followed by a bigger right hand dropped Billy for the count of six. Gus was right on him as he arose, and four left hooks set up a plastering right that dropped Fox for the full ten count.

Fox now had 52 fights; he won 50 by knockout and lost two by knockout, both to the Cliffside Park, New Jersey, champion. Lesnevich had reached the pinnacle of his career. Sol Strauss, the new Garden matchmaker, was after Gus to challenge Joe Louis for the heavyweight title. Gus told him more than once he didn't want a Louis bout. As before stated, Gus was the honest workman. He knew he couldn't give Louis 30-odd pounds and have any chance against the Bomber. Why BS the fans?

After the early kayo of Billy Fox, Lesnevich was the buzz of the boxing world. In an interview with *Ring* magazine writer and artist Ted Carroll, Ted sized Gus up as "pleasant mannered, friendly and articulate. Gus is an interviewer's delight." Ted described Gus well. In an article written by Gus himself, he delivers it all in one nutshell. The following is in Gus's own words: "I was not a great fighter in my own eyes. I did not become a great puncher until the tail end of my career, when I lost some of my speed and came down off my toes and punched flat-footed. Then I started to hit real well. Before that I was only a fair puncher, fair boxer. But no one wanted to win more than I did. I was lucky enough to have a hard head and chin. Although I was stopped five times, it was cuts that did me in."

Well put, honest Gus. Over the years, such modesty has become nonexistent in our athletes. Here was a man who, although becoming a world famous champion, never left his small town of Cliffside Park, New Jersey, a down-to-earth family man. He never needed an oversized hat.

Billy Fox never did reach the heights some people predicted he would. After the second Lesnevich kayo, he suffered. Literally. His fearless team threw him to the wolves. His opponents were no longer carefully picked. He was knocked out four more times before calling it a career. Believe it or not, Fox was finished, a worn-out fighter at the age of 24. Was it poor management?

Billy could punch hard; he had that big gun just like an army tank. But even the tank has armor around the main gun, and also smaller guns and personnel to maneuver its body inside and outside of enemy fire. The tank also had mechanics looking out after its condition and well-being. Billy Fox stood alone. He had no one looking out for him.

Gus's manager, Joe Vella, while contemplating his fighter's next opponent, was again offered a big-money fight in England. The Brits wanted Freddy Mills to do it again with Gus. In their first fight, Mills was coming on when he was suddenly knocked out in a great match, as previously mentioned. Vella and Gus made another end run around Ezz Charles and Archie Moore, the number one and two contenders for Gus's title. For the 33-year-old Gus's time ran out. He took a beating from ferocious Mills and was lucky to last the 15 rounds. His title gone, Gus came back to the States dejected. The year was 1948.

In July of the next year he would fight for the NBA heavyweight title facing the man who succeeded the retired Joe Louis. Ezzard Charles had recently won that title, and for his first defense he picked Gus Lesnevich as his challenger, proving Ezz never had any ill feelings against Gus or his manager Joe Vella for giving both Freddy Mills and Billy Fox two shots each while avoiding Ezz. That's boxing, and Ezz understood the money had to be made when the opportunity presented itself.

In August of 1949 Gus challenged Ezzard Charles for the heavyweight title at Yankee Stadium. It was all Charles, as the younger, faster man sharpshooted his way to a seventh-round stoppage. Gus, after taking a beating for the first five rounds, with eye cuts and swelling of both optics, went all out in the sixth. In a last-ditch stand, Gus rocked Ezzard with a series of right-hand bombs in a go-for-broke effort. That was the only round Gus won. In the seventh Ezz picked up where he left off in the fifth and pelted Gus plenty. Joe Vella refused to let Gus continue. He couldn't watch Gus take such a beating in a fight he couldn't win. Lesnevich retired after this fight. He knew it was time to hang 'em up.

Years later, their fighting careers over, the Lion and the Fox would meet again. Gus recalled this meeting to boxing writers. Lesnevich and a few friends decided to go bowling and stopped at an alley near Philadelphia. They rolled a few games had some cold brews, and as they were finishing up, the pin setter (pin boy) approached. He came up to get the bowlers' score sheets and tip; it would be his proof to the establishment that he set up their games, thus getting credit at pay time.

As Gus handed the sheets over to the young man, they startled each other. The pin boy recognized the bowler as Gus Lesnevich, former light heavyweight champion of the world. Lesnevich finally saw that his pin boy of the night was none other than his two-time challenger for his title, Black Jack Billy from Philly, Billy Fox.

Lesnevich didn't know Fox was the pin setter because looking down the alley he saw a young man wearing glasses with heavy Coke-bottle lenses. Fox didn't know Gus was bowling because he couldn't see that far from his position in the "pits."

Both were very happy to see each other and reminisce about their title fights. But the fact remained, Gus was still the pitcher and Fox the catcher. Gus threw hard with boxing gloves as well as bowling balls. Lesnevich was always a very generous man. Fox probably got the best tip of his pin-setter career that night.

Gus after his retirement from the ring was fairly comfortable financially. He was still in boxing as a referee and guest speaker. Fox fell on hard times and wound up scraping out a living any way he could. It was tough with failing eyesight.

Strange how two well-known moneymaking fighters' trails would lead in different directions. Was it poor management? Joe Vella was Gus Lesnevich's manager. Fox had the team of Blinkey Palermo and Frankie Carbo as his managers. Enough said.

The last time your writer saw Gus was December 14, 1962, at Totowa's Gladiators Arena, later known as Ice World. Gus was the referee for the main event, one that promised to be a very good one. Joe Williams, a top New Jersey amateur star and now a hot pro prospect, was taking on the very capable Stephan Redl. It was a huge step up for Williams. This would be his first main event, and many believed he bit off more than he could chew by facing the rough tough Redl so early in his career. Sitting at ringside, my friends and I settled back to enjoy Williams's test "by fire." The opening bell and both men engaged in heavy trading exchanges. Midway in the round, Redl came out of a clinch with blood pouring down his face. It was a bad cut above the eye, a clash of heads. The referee took a good look and stopped the fight. Everyone in the arena was angry and disappointed in the quick finish of the fight. Gus Lesnevich, the referee, was booed and cursed by *some* ingrates at ringside. What these fools didn't know was Gus's feelings on stopping a fight on facial cuts. Lesnevich knew that kind of heartbreak because he lived it more than once himself. You could tell by his body language how much he detested stopping the fight. If there was one person in that arena who didn't want it stopped more than Gus, that was Stephan Redl. With the head-butt rule not in effect at that time, Redl lost by first-round TKO. The only people celebrating in that building were Joe Williams and his handlers. Gus was the undeserved villain even though he did the right thing. The cut was of such a nature that for Redl to continue would be flirting with permanent eye damage. Gus took the boos, curses and criticism like the man that he was—one of class. Could anyone suggest, "What fools these mortals be?" About 15 months later Gus died of a heart attack. He had just turned 49.

Gus's early demise stunned his many fans and the world of boxing. The sport had lost one of its true role models. The blue-collar champion, New Jersey's own.

Best Wins

Alabama Kid	KO9
Lou Brouillard	W10
Bob Olin	W12
Dave Clark	KO1
Nathan Mann	W10
Anton Christoforidis	W15
Tami Mauriello	W15
Joe Kahut	KO1
Freddy Mills	KO10
Billy Fox	KO10
Melio Bettina	KO1
Tami Mauriello	KO7
Billy Fox	KO1

The Staircase to
Boxing's Fond Memories

Memories and corners, as in the song so beautifully sung by Barbra Streisand, will be our topic.

Anyone in love with boxing as the writer is has four corners in the mind, much like a boxing ring. The corners are used for storage of fond memories of boxers, the places where they fought and trained, and of course the results of their fights. Those memories can bring back the best times of one's life with a few jogs. Just like starting a lawn mower. "The Way We Were." The song goes on.

In recent correspondence with Tommy Kaczmarek, the all-time greatest and most respected of boxing judges, we both recalled a place fond to both our minds. The gym in the basement of the Elizabeth Recreation Center. It was first known by Elizabeth youth as Midtown Community Center, and later called Kirk Center, named after James T. Kirk who was elected and reelected numerous times as Elizabeth, New Jersey, mayor. Tom's jog opened this "place," one of the most cherished of my youth, to my favorite pastime, reminiscing back to the golden olden days of New Jersey boxing. Way, way back to the late 1940s and early 1950s.

The Center is located in Peterstown, the Italian section of Elizabeth. This small gym was something out of a Hollywood movie script, only better. The Academy Award–winning movie *Million Dollar Baby* could have used the Midtown Gym. It was more realistic than the one used in the film.

The Center was of course financed by the city of Elizabeth, the money just enough to keep the place running. The city couldn't go elaborate; they had the taxpayers to contend with. Little did they know at the time that the frugal sum spent for the center helped shape hundreds of young men's lives. It kept them off the streets and out of trouble, getting them into sports and thereby instilling pride in themselves and helping them learn to live and play by the rules of life that are not to be broken. A small investment indeed for aiding those kids in becoming solid law-abiding citizens.

One can never forget the first walk off the main floor at the Kirk Community Center to the rickety flight of wooden steps that squeaked and groaned as we followed them down to the boxing gym. The air was filled with the odor of liniment and sweat. It wasn't an unpleasant odor; it was what a real gym should smell like. This walk I would repeat many times in the future. When entering the gym, the boxing ring was on the immediate right, set in a corner. Wooden floorboards covered with canvas were set against the concrete floor. Four ring posts held the ring ropes in place. The ropes were thought to be very old since they had yards and yards of adhesive taped wrapped around their entire length for support from age and wear. Wooden benches could be placed on only two sides of the ring for the viewers. The other two sides were against the wall, as the ring was set in the corner. The ring canvas was dirty from all the use it got. One seam was taped over more than once. I imagined most of the spots on that canvas were bloodstains. Raggedy-tag but useable. Along the far wall were cream-colored metal lockers, all with their locking mechanisms broken, but again still useable. While working out, a fighter had a place to put his street clothes and wallet, but he had to keep on constant alert that the little kids who frequented the gym kept their hands off.

Long wooden benches were placed in front of the lockers. One lone rubbing table was available, and a full-length mirror was hung for shadow boxing use. Two heavy bags, their canvas worn thin from the punches received, hung from the ceiling on chains. One speed-bag rack was there for those who had a speed bag. It seemed only the pro fighters could afford such a luxury. A small shower room with two showerheads was in constant use as the fighters came and went. Steam constantly came out of the open door. Above the gym was the basketball court, which was always in use through the evening. It supplied a constant rumble to the already noisy gym. Both sounds suggested huge youthful activity. Much energy burned, at the right time and place.

Forever encased in my mind is the memory of my first visit to "Kirk Center" gym. The first sight I saw was two fighters going at it hammer and tong in a spirited sparring session. I immediately sat down on a bench only a few feet away from the action. I was never that close to ring action before, and it scared me a bit. The power and viciousness of the punches were shocking to this young boy who would get used to it soon enough.

I could see that these guys were professionals; they were very good. Both fighters were wearing headgear and protective cups. I noticed the initials T.K. on one fighter's headgear. Then I recognized Tommy Kaczmarek, a local pro whom I had seen fight at Twin City Bowl. As they continued to spar, I finally made out Tom's opponent. He was Tic Mollozzi, a Carmen Basilio–type of fighter, known as the "South Street Slugger" by Elizabeth, New Jersey, fight fans. I'd also seen Tic fight, and he was strictly punch and destroy.

My first time behind the scenes seeing the fighters train remains vivid in my mind. It was just as exciting as being at the Twin City or Elizabeth Armory fights. I would later learn that some if not many gym workouts are more vicious and hard fought than the real thing. Tic and Tommy's workouts were no exception.

The gym became one of my favorite places. Some of the finest people your writer would ever meet were found at Kirk Center. The noisy wooden steps had been entrance and exit for many great fighters along with just plain good folks.

The main man at the gym was Tony Orlando, Sr. He was the unsalaried boxing director and trainer. Tony, a former pro boxer, gave much of his life to boxing. For many years he was known as the man to see if one was interested in becoming a boxer, amateur or pro. He never turned anyone away. Tony took on any kid that wanted to push leather. It is said that he never took a penny from his pro fighters for his services or time. Tony *was* Elizabeth, New Jersey, boxing. Some of the punch-for-pay boys he trained were Freddy Russo, Roger Murial, Charley Slaughter and Richie Gonzalez, to name a few.

In 1949 and 1950, Kirk Center was bustling with ring activity. The *Elizabeth Daily Journal* had sponsored the Union County Diamond Gloves Tournament. Hundreds of kids from all over town and the county signed up. Kirk Center would accommodate most of them. They needed trainers, and the old-time Elizabeth boxers answered the call. All good men. They became teachers of the manly art as well as fathers away from home to the young pugilists. Headed by Tony Orlando, Sr., were Mickey Bellaro, Joe "TNT" Tinarella, Rocky Albano, Gene Holmes, Willie Robinson, Joe Orsini, Johnny Baltz, Mickey Greb and Joe Harris. Pete Nozza was the youngest of the trainers and also an excellent one. These men really cared for their fighters.

Tommy Kaczmarek always claimed that Joe Harris, who trained Tommy as an amateur and pro, was a milestone in Tommy's life that taught and always stressed gentlemanly behavior along with clean living. Tom is a shining example of that.

There was an acquaintance of mine who wanted to enter the Diamond Gloves that year. He had never had a pair of boxing gloves on in his life. He mentioned to the priest at his parish that he needed a good trainer. The priest knew one of his longtime parishioners had a boxing background. He got the novice boxer together with Joe Harris, the old pro. Just four weeks of training under Harris got the 135-pounder his first of five wins in a division packed with talent that year. Joe Oliveri, the drummer boy, was the hero of the tournament. His wins were action packed and title winning. Oliveri then joined the Marines and won the All-Marine Championship at Paris Island. Harris did wonders for that kid. It proved his ability as a top-notch trainer.

Other gyms around town also had excellent trainers, so the competition was fierce. The Diamond Gloves was a huge success for the city of Elizabeth and Union County. The big winner of course was boxing itself. Everyone was talking boxing; it was a good feeling. The Diamond Gloves were held for two years by the *Elizabeth Daily Journal*. Both years the Kirk Center, aka Elizabeth Rec, took the team championship.

Many years later, my then four-year-old granddaughter's preschool class put on a play. It was to be held at Kirk Center. It was news to her grandparents that "Kirk" was still open and running. We had moved from that area years before. Grandparents were invited to attend the play, and we were very happy to go along. As soon as we were seated, I just had to slip away to check out the gym. It was the evening hours, and as I approached the gym stairs, they were lighted up with a night-light. As I descended, the squeaking and groaning sound was heard again, the first time for me in *40 years*. The same stairs, the same sound.

It was hard to believe, but I loved every second of that great symphony, a melody for fistiana. Talk about jogging fond memories.

The gym was dark; the doors were closed and ribboned off. Everything had a fresh coat of paint. Missing was the pungent odors of sweat and liniment. If they were there, it would have made things complete, as if going back in time.

Squeaking, groaning wooden staircases became very familiar to your writer. They first came to my attention at the Elizabeth Armory when attending fights there. Laurel Garden also had a pair of musical stairs. Kirk Center had the very best of the three for their haunting strains of the sweet science. They became part of my boxing memories. Of the three establishments, only Midtown-Kirk is still standing. Hopefully that staircase is still there. The sound they created is never to be forgotten by this boxing fan. To me it became a gateway to thousands of fond memories of every boxer who ever trained there.

Upon checking at the office, we were told the gym was closed for the summer months. And yes, of course, the fighters always had to switch their workouts to Warinanco Park Stadium because the gym was not air-conditioned. We were told at this period of time that the gym was still cranking out the best amateur fighters, but nothing like the early fifties when boxing was king in Elizabeth and all of New Jersey. Pro boxing had left the city. All the great trainers were long gone. Good jobs were now available, and not as many kids got involved in boxing.

After such a long absence, the place looked better than ever. That told me the city did find out the value of the Center to its youth. It helped me as a youngster, and even now my granddaughter was using the facility as a preschooler. May the Elizabeth Recreation Center long exist, and thank you, Tommy Kaczmarek, for jogging these fond memories from the corners of my mind of that special place.

Professional Fighters Who Graced the "Kirk" Gym in the Late '40s and Early '50s

1. Phil Saxton
2. Gene "Ace" Armstrong
3. Harold Carter
4. Dom Zimbardo
5. Pearce Patton

6. Tommy Kaczmarek
7. Gene Bora
8. Dominick "Tic" Molozzi
9. Freddy Conn
10. Clint Miller
11. Lenny LaBrutta
12. Roger Murial
13. Frankie Duane
14. Birdie Loffa
15. Freddy Russo
16. Pete Yellowvich
17. Gene Washington
18. Charley Slaughter
19. George Howard
20. James Patrick Ryan
21. Kid Sharkey
22. Al Diaz
23. Jimmy Esposito
24. Freddy Hermann
25. Country Sherman

*The amateurs were too numerous to mention.

Joe Frazier:
Deceiving First Appearances

Smoking Joe Frazier was a ruggedly built heavyweight boxer. When he was smoking, he reminded me of a runaway train. His aggressiveness was awesome. I first saw Joe in 1964, the year he was picked to represent America in the Olympics in Japan. Up until that time I never heard of him.

While a member of the Trenton, New Jersey, boxing team, he came to my hometown to compete in our state's Golden Gloves, the tournament being held at our local Elks Club in Elizabeth, New Jersey.

I had talked two of my fellow workers into accompanying me to the fights. It would be their first time seeing boxing live and up close. We took ringside seats, and I had to answer what seemed like a million questions before, during and after each fight all night long. The final fight of the night would be an open-class heavyweight bout.

The two fighters entered the ring, and I immediately recognized Gerald O'Neil, a very good Jersey amateur heavyweight I had seen before. I looked at his smaller, squat opponent and felt sorry for him. I told my friends to get ready for a slaughter in this terrible mismatch. This unknown Philly fighter was about to get his "head knocked off," was my prediction. If appearances won fights, the muscular, well-proportioned O'Neil was a shoo-in over his smaller fireplug-looking rival.

The first-round bell hadn't faded away when a terrible ferocious left hook bounced off O'Neil's jaw and dropped him like a sack of potatoes. My ego was flattened like O'Neil lying in the prone position before our eyes. My friends were laughing at me for the huge buildup I had bestowed on the downed fighter. After calling the shots all night, my finale was a disaster. Somehow, almost miraculously, O'Neil scraped his way off the canvas at the count of nine. He bravely weathered the expected storm from his steamroller opponent. Midway into the second round we could have used the words made famous by Howard Cosell years later: "Down goes Frazier, down goes Frazier." For he was. O'Neil smashed Joe to the canvas with a crackling right hand, returning the favor. Joe was lucky to finish the round. He took a pasting in the third and lost the decision. O'Neil had vindicated himself and yours truly. I regained my friends' confidence in me as an amateur boxing authority.

I was, however, stunned by Frazier's performance. "Where the hell did this guy come from?" was my thought. Some months later on a Saturday afternoon I stumbled upon the Olympic boxing trials on TV. I recall that the fights were held at the Singer Bowl in New York City. I was surprised to see Joe Frazier again. He was paired with a guy who looked twice his size. The fellow was a huge blob; he had to be over 300 pounds. (Heavyweight weights are not announced in amateur fights.) I figured Frazier with that terrible left hook of his would punch holes in this Pillsbury Doughboy.

Frazier got his ears boxed off and lost the decision. The Doughboy's name was Buster Mathis, who would beat Frazier again in the second box-off to win the right to represent the United States in the upcoming Olympics. I wrote Joe Frazier off. After all, he had lost to O'Neil and soft-punching Buster Mathis *twice*. His only consolation was he was picked to be Buster's alternate in Tokyo, Japan.

In a cycle of events that would make Hollywood scripts read anemic, Joe Frazier would meet his fate that destiny willed to him. Collections by his friends and neighbors were taken to help finance Joe's trip to Japan and keep his wife and children secure till he returned to Philly. Things got better, much better, for Joe, but not for Buster Mathis, who broke his right hand in prepping for the Olympics. As alternate, Joe was catapulted into the games as our heavyweight hopeful for gold.

After the three aforementioned losses, Joe took it to the limit. *He won the gold medal.* Talk about underdogs.

On his triumphant return to the States, he signed a lucrative pro contract. Joe Frazier became famous, a household name, a millionaire and a Hall of Fame superstar. He will forever be joined with Muhammad Ali for their trilogy of great fights.

Who would ever believe that the unknown fighter lying in the rosin dust on that canvas in the Elks Club that night years before would become heavyweight champion of the world. Fate, destiny, whatever you would call it. I think first appearances are deceiving, after all.

Gerald O'Neil, a winner, faded from the scene, Buster Mathis would fight Joe Frazier again as pros in a title match for part of Muhammad Ali's vacated crown. He was annihilated by Joe, who went on to defeat Ali for all the marbles.

Time and time again boxing proves it's a sport for underdogs. It brings out just what a human being can do if he puts his body and soul into it.

Tony Riccio:
The Tungsten Steel Man

When the list of inductees for the November 1, 2006, New Jersey Boxing Hall of Fame was released, I was pleasantly surprised to see the name Tony Riccio. Not that Tony didn't belong. Hell, it was long overdue. I was eager to meet him.

My surprise was, and with the greatest respect for Tony, let me say this, I saw Tony fight many times long years ago. I didn't think he was still with us in this year 2006. I honestly thought his style of never-ending punching, plus fighting none but the best (his total number of pro fights over 100), would have shortened his life span.

All but four or five of his fights went the distance, with Tony punching from bell to bell. With only a handful of knockouts to his credit, no puncher was Tony. He won by burying his opponents in his hell-bent-for-leather style. No wonder he was burned out at age 24. Going the distance in his many main events was brutal even on this iron man. He was such a crowd-pleaser that the promoters were after him all the time. They knew that Tony could draw a crowd and give the customer *action*.

Fearless, he took on champions and number-one contenders and gave them all a battle. His record is full of all the top names of his day. His selection to the New Jersey Boxing Hall of Fame warrants a gold medal to that selecting committee.

A true Jersey fighter from Bayonne, a city that produced many Jersey greats, Tony, and his nemesis Joe Curcio, kept Jersey fight arenas buzzing in the '40s and early '50s.

Your writer was always amazed by these two Italian-American warriors. They would fight anyone, bar none, and go out there to annihilate their opponents. When they ran out of tough guys to fight, they fought each other. None could be tougher than they themselves were for a Gatti-Ward kind of fight. They clashed *six times*, Curcio winning four, Tony Riccio winning two. All crowd-pleasing fights.

Some of the fighters Tony won over were such stalwarts as the former lightweight champion Sammy Angott (the first man to beat the great Willie Pep), Jackie Wilson, Sonny Horne and Norman Rubio (twice). A draw with number-one ranked middleweight contender Rocky Castellani was by no means a small feat at age 19. He gave Sugar Ray Robinson a battle for four rounds in my hometown armory in February of 1946, giving everything he had.

Check this list of who's who in boxing at the time. Tony gave them all hell, win or lose: Aaron Perry, Freddy Archer, Izzy Jannazzo, Cecil Hudson, Pete Mead, Buster Tyler, Lee Sala, Danny Kapilow, Tommy Parks, Charley Fusari, George Small, Tommy Bell, Joe Miceli, and Mike DeCosmo. Stalwarts, yes indeed.

On the night of November 1, 2006, Tony showed up for his induction, and that is where I met one of my boyhood boxing favorites. Tony was born August 30, 1926, so he was 80 years old but didn't look it. Tony was well dressed in a business suit. He looked to be a few pounds over the last weight he fought at, junior middleweight. He had a full head of gray hair, and his face was still handsome, notwithstanding the many wars he engaged in. He looked great. Many younger people at this, the 37th Annual Induction Dinner of the New Jersey Boxing Hall of Fame, did not know who he was. Soon the word was passed around the tables that this man, Tony Riccio, had fought the great Sugar Ray Robinson in Robby's heyday. Doesn't that speak volumes for boxing's greatest ever?

Tony sat at the head table with the rest of the inductees who were all being approached for autographs. My wife and daughter tried to get Tony's signature, but to no avail. Tony wasn't signing autographs this night. The person sitting next to him told the signature seekers Tony was confused and didn't know what they wanted. He also was a man of few words. I guess old age and the hundred-odd fights he had did take a toll on Tony, yet he appeared and acted normal. Maybe the old gent just didn't like signing autographs.

At evening's end as the people were filing out, with some stragglers in spots still talking boxing, I spotted Tony Riccio. He was still sitting at the same but now empty table. I figured I got him alone. How could he refuse me an autograph? Well, he did. He pushed away my program booklet. I set it back down on the table next to him.

Paul Venti, president of the New Jersey IVBA Ring 25, was standing nearby. I went over to talk with him, purposely leaving Riccio alone with my program, hoping he would sign it. Every time I talked boxing with Paul, we got carried away. We were so engrossed in our conversation I forgot about the autograph.

Suddenly I saw Tony Riccio walking toward us. As he was passing by, I told Paul Venti, "That's Tony Riccio; he fought Joe Curcio *five* times." Venti nodded to me; as he did, Riccio took one step back and growled, "Six times." Paul and I got a chuckle out of that. We both agreed there's nothing wrong with Tony even if he won't sign autographs. I went back to retrieve my program from where I left it. I looked at the page his story and photo were on. He didn't sign it. I said good evening to Paul Venti. We both agreed Tony Riccio is some stubborn guy, with a sharp memory.

A few days later as I read that program from cover to cover, I found it. Tony had signed it. He ever so neatly wrote his name on his photo across the chest. The photo was a bit gray in color around the chest area, so one had to look close to see the signature. He again proved his class, as he did in his entire boxing career.

It was indeed a great night for Tony and me and the other inductees. On a sad note, though, it was the last time I would ever see or converse with Paul Venti. He passed away a few months later. Boxing lost one of its best.

Al Guido:
The Measuring Man

Always used as the opponent, Al was tough and skilled enough to give any up-and-coming prospect a good test. It was worth getting a win over Guido to enhance the youngster's resume and extend his win streak. Guido lacked a KO punch, so the young ones were pretty well insured from any upset kayo loss. Promoters used Guido often. Beat Guido and you had possibilities.

Why write about Al Guido? Indeed, a very unlikely fighter to write about. True, but with a deeper check of the record books, I found in his resume very remarkable and interesting issues. His career spanned the years 1940 to 1951. He never fought for the title, nor was he ever rated in the top ten.

He fought all the top fighters of that time period in his weight division. He fought 98 times, an average of nine fights per year—unheard of by today's standards. Another thing that caught my eye was the fact that he was stopped only once; that loss came in his fourth pro fight to a fighter who had lost both of his previous fights and was winless. It could have been a cut eye or other injury because the durable Guido never came close to a kayo defeat in his next *94* fights, many against top contenders.

Another look at the records shows Guido scored only 11 knockouts in his entire career. He lost 35 on points, and the most incredible statistic is the fact that he fought *16 draws*. Going over numerous records, I haven't seen any fighter with that many even fights. One reason for all the draws could be that Guido was not endowed with charisma or dashing ways; his personality had a lot to be desired. He entered the ring looking like a loser and appeared shopworn. He wasn't handsome or popular. He looked the part of the villain. All this plays on the mind of some young inexperienced judges. The draw verdict would save the favorite from defeat and keep the fans happy. Anyway, who cared about Al Guido? He was a loser.

That's the point of this story. I'm in defense of losers who gave their all. They are essential in our sport. They shouldn't be frowned upon or ridiculed by the fans or writers trying to be boxing writers who think they know boxing but in reality know very little of the "sweet science." Guido in losing always gave his very best and gave a rough meaningful fight to his opponent.

Guido's biggest win was scored over a streaking Tony Janiro at MSG. He halted Tony's streak at 23 for Janiro's first loss. Janiro, whom boxing writers were calling the second Tony Canzaneri, had Hollywood good looks, was very young and had a beautiful boxing style. A superb boxer. When he first came on the scene, the Garden promoters immediately made him a "house fighter." The fans loved him. He was so popular that he was put into a Garden main event scheduled for *eight* rounds, which was a first and set a record. He was too young to fight ten rounds—the New York Boxing Commission's rule.

A fan of Janiro's was Harry S Truman, the vice president of the United States. Many old-timers will recall the famous photo of Truman shaking the young fighter's hand as he left the ring after scoring another victory. Back in the dressing room, the kid told his trainers, "Ya know, I just shook hands with the vice president of the *Garden*." Reporters interviewing Tony cracked up laughing.

Needless to say, the upset of Tony Janiro was Guido's biggest win.

Guido fought in my hometown, Elizabeth, New Jersey, six times. He managed an eight-round decision victory over our neighborhood fighter Freddie Herman.

Your writer attended Guido's next-to-last fight of his career. He took on Tony Janiro at Twin City Bowl and lost the ten-round decision in a spirited fight. It was his fourth fight with Janiro. Other top-ten contenders he fought multiple times were Billy Graham, 0 for 3, and Bobby Ruffin, 0 for 4. All good, hard-fought fights, proving that Guido was only one short step away from being a contender himself.

According to the record books, his last fight was with Chico Vejar, a hot prospect. Again the same scenario. Chico entered the ring with 25 starts. He would leave the ring 26–0 after a hard-fought eight rounds. He passed his test and gained needed experience and remained undefeated.

Guido measured Vejar well, letting the matchmakers and promoters know Vejar had the goods to go on to many lucrative television fights, which he did. The fight left Vejar happy with the win, and the fans happy with the action provided. Everyone made money, and Guido could look forward to plenty of work battling the coming future stars and supplying them with rigid tests.

Sadly, all would change. What makes this story unique is the fact that Guido had one more unscheduled fight with his wife, and lost. For reasons of her own, she placed the barrel of a pistol in his ear as he took his afternoon nap and pulled the trigger. Guido was down and out and finally kayoed after 94 fights.

The best fighters in the world during an 11-year span tried and failed to keep him down. He was truly a great measuring stick of their ability and punch.

Losers, if very competitive and durable, are a much-needed ingredient in our sport. Yes, they could make a profitable career of it as Al Guido did. A look at his dismal losing record can turn one off. But on second focus, one can admire all he contributed to the sport of boxing. Sixteen draws—amazing. A true "blue-collar" fighter.

Chuck Wepner:
The Red Badge of Courage

A number of wannabe boxing writers, in their inept attempt at trying to be "cute" and assume the role of comedians, "branded" Chuck Wepner with the "Bayonne Bleeder" tag. They sarcastically wrote that Chuck would start bleeding as he received the last-minute rule instructions in ring center before the first-round bell. Some people enjoyed the joke; many others took it (the name) as an insult. If those writers wanted so badly to become comedians, they should have joined the circus as clowns. My answer to them is one large Bronx cheer.

It should sound like the familiar "passing of gas" sound. Yes, the name "Bronx cheer" originated in New York. The old-timers used it extensively at major league baseball games against the umpires. Naturally it filtered its way into all sporting events and beyond. It truly became popular and famous. So I offer those responsible for the moniker bestowed on Chuck not one but three huge Bronx cheer salutes.

Your writer may be wrong in his belief, but I can recall a very good fighter named Gene Hairston who was deaf and was labeled Gene "Dummy" Hairston by the boxing writers. How do you think that kid felt when seeing it in print? When Hairston made the big time, headlining Madison Square Garden cards fighting Jake LaMotta, Kid Gavilan, etc., the real, true boxing writers saw to it that the fighter's name and future introductions would be Gene "Silent" Hairston. They did the right thing. People with class do not call a cripple a "gimp" or a person with lung disease a "lunger," etc. Anyway, I dislike that name they call Chuck.

Wepner couldn't help the fact that he was prone to cuts. To me he showed his great courage by fighting through many of his blood-spattered fights. I like to refer to Chuck as the Red Badge of *Courage*, a much more suitable, truly appropriate name for such a gallant warrior.

New Jersey and its boxing fans could all be proud of Chuck for his never-give-up attitude and never being in a dull fight.

I first heard and saw Chuck on TV in the early 1960s. He had entered the New York Golden Gloves and fought his way up to the finals of the novice heavyweight division. The finals were televised from Madison Square Garden. Chuck and his opponent were billed as both former Marines. If my memory serves me right, his opponent's last name was Sullivan, although I wouldn't bank on it. If indeed there were two former Marines in there that night, they certainly bestowed much pride on the Corp. In a blazing shootout Pier 6 brawl, Chuck won the decision and the Golden Glove novice heavyweight title. From that point on Chuck was beloved by both New Jersey and Big Apple boxing fans. Chuck was already in his mid-twenties, so he didn't linger in the amateurs.

Little did he know he would become a fixture in Madison Square Garden and its smaller arena, Felt Forum, after turning pro. When he retired after 14 years of punching for pay, he was honored by the Garden with a Chuck Wepner Night Fight Card and presented with a lifetime golden ticket to all future Garden fights. It was a kind of payback for all the thrills he provided the Garden customers over a decade.

I could never understand why Wepner never had his autobiography written or Hollywood do a full-scale movie on him. I know a few TV documentaries were done, but they didn't focus on his complete story.

It's my belief he lived a very adventurous life, and at this writing still is. Chuck by no means was a choirboy. As a youth he was rough and tough; he became a noted barroom brawler and street fighter, then a bouncer. He traveled with a rough crowd and could handle himself well. I believe this led to his taking up boxing. Chuck's dad was also a pro fighter, so the seeds were sown.

Other interesting activities he engaged in besides his Marine Corps stint included his time playing semi-pro basketball; they say he was very good at it. He took a job as a security guard at Western Electric and held that job until his ring notoriety landed him a job as a liquor salesman for a nationally known company. His popularity lifted all sales on the route assigned to him.

When Chuck started his pro career, by no means was he coddled by his management. In his fifth pro fight, he was matched with Ray Patterson, a hot prospect and brother of Floyd. Chuck won the decision.

Wepner was tall and rangy; he was not a clever boxer or a huge puncher. I'd describe him as a mauler with a clubbing right hand who applied constant pressure roughing up his opponents. He used the tools he had, and he used them well to his advantage. He also possessed a granite jaw, which certainly helped him in slugging matches with the world's best. He was stopped nine times, mostly from facial cuts. Muhammad Ali, Sonny Liston, and George Foreman were the heavyweight champions Chuck faced, along with top contenders Ernie Terrell, Joe Bugner, Duane Bobick, Manuel Ramos, Scott Frank, Joe "King" Roman, Randy Neumann and Buster Mathis, quite a gallery of tough guys.

There was a saying heard many times, "Everybody likes Chuck Wepner," and so it was, as his career moved along, people liked the way he never bragged or boasted, never bad mouthed his opponents, and would not use the so called "trash talk" that is so popular with some fighters. He was the big teddy bear with the cowboy hat to his fans.

In 1967 Chuck scored a good win over Don McAteer for the New Jersey state heavyweight title. In 1968 he took on Forest Ward, a fine prospect being groomed by Madison Square Garden. Chuck stopped him in the seventh round. That got Chuck a fight in Puerto Rico with Joe "King" Roman, a rated heavyweight. Chuck lost a ten-round decision, one of five decisions he would lose in a 51-fight career.

In 1970 I believe Chuck fought the greatest fight of his career. He was matched with highly rated Manuel Ramos, the heavyweight champ of Mexico who had recently given heavyweight champion Joe Frazier two rounds of pure hell in a world title fight at the Garden.

These two gladiators met in ring center at the first-round bell and started blazing away, throwing punches in bunches. Both being very proud fighters, neither one would back away, and so it went round after round; no quarter was asked or given.

In the fifth round, I looked down on the ring. The fight I thought was about even, but Chuck had numerous facial cuts. His head looked like a large, bright red tomato sitting on top of a fair-skinned body. The contrast was frightening. Chuck's whole head was soaked with blood. Yes, including his scalp. The crowd was roaring, and I feared Chuck once again would be stopped on cuts. It would be a pity if it was, because no man should fight that hard and valiantly only to lose.

I was surprised to see the ref let it go into round six. Al Bravermann and Co. did a fine job curtailing some of the blood flow. Any other fighter would have gone into a defensive mode trying to avoid the punches to protect the cuts and avoid a stoppage, with focus on lasting the ten rounds and losing the decision.

That motive never entered Chuck's mind; it was simply not part of his makeup. To him that kind of thinking doesn't belong in a true warrior's mental arsenal. I was worried; his corner was worried, as were many fans. One person wasn't—Chuck himself. He was used to fighting through a mask of blood, and he kept punching away as he did in the first five rounds.

Into round nine, and the pace never slowed. The crowd was delirious, with Wepner fans and a large number of Latinos going nuts.

As the bell ended the ten-rounder, both battlers were still clubbing away. Chuck got the nod. Both fighters had to be in top shape to produce such a great memorable battle. In my ledger of all-time great heavyweight fights, it made the top ten.

It's my belief that on that given night, January 26, 1970, Chuck fought his greatest fight. Many fighters experience such a happening as Chuck did. Of the rated top-ten heavies of that day, I dare say that on that night Chuck would have beaten any one of them, with the exception of Muhammad Ali and Joe Frazier, and even those champs would know they were in a battle.

The Ramos win earned Chuck a fight with the former champion, the feared Sonny Liston, "Mr. Loveable," who was attempting a comeback. The fight would take place at Jersey City Armory. Chuck was delighted. He hustled ticket buyers on his liquor salesman route and boosted his purse to $10,000, plus a promise that the winner would get a shot at top contender Jerry Quarry at the Garden.

Chuck even wrote letters to the New Jersey Boxing Commission requesting tolerant officials who didn't mind some blood, letting it be known he would bleed in this fight.

Liston had a booming right hand and a long, very powerful left jab that landed like a battering ram. It seemed he couldn't miss Chuck with it that blood-soaked night. The referee was very tolerant. Chuck started bleeding early all the way to the final tenth round. The ref, the ring, and the ringside spectators were all splattered with blood. Some fans were hollering to the ref to stop the fight. Chuck was behind on points anyway. So the third man did his duty and called it off. It was reported that Chuck received over 50 sutures to close his facial wounds. When reporters asked the always-scowling Liston how come he couldn't knock out the tough Wepner and wasn't he brave staying in to the tenth and final round. Liston replied, "He ain't brave; his manager is."

It would be Liston's last fight. A few months later he was found dead in his Las Vegas hotel room of suspicious circumstances.

The Liston fight, although a loss for Chuck, only added to Chuck's popularity. Boxing fans were amazed at Chuck's staying power, even against one of boxing's all-time murderous punchers. After all, the facts remained; Liston, a huge favorite, could not floor the Bayonne strong boy but had to settle for a TKO win on cuts.

English fight fans were salivating over their new heavyweight sensation. Young Joe Bugner was over 200 pounds and well over six feet tall. A big, blond, handsome boxer-puncher was being groomed to become world champion. His management was choosing his opponents carefully, making sure the huge Adonis had the edge in each fight. With over 25 wins under his belt, it was time to match him with a world-class foe.

Why not Chuck Wepner, whose recent fight with Liston enhanced his marketability and notoriety? Chuck hightailed it over to England looking forward to engaging their new hero.

The fight was stopped in the third round. The newspapers called it a premature stoppage. As soon as the ref saw blood over Chuck's eye, he called a halt. I think the Brit's idea was, "Why take a chance? Let's get this dangerous Bayonne Bull out of the China shop before he can cause any damage." It secured a big-name win on Bugner's resume. Wepner was furious; he took the English officials to task for the early stoppage, claiming he was cut worse while shaving. Chuck lost little prestige from this fight; every fan knew he was right. (Note: Bugner went on to take Ali and Joe Frazier the distance in decision losses to them. Ali twice. Neither one could even floor the tough Brit.)

Wepner's team decided it was time to defend his New Jersey state heavyweight title. As top New Jersey contender, Randy Neumann was selected. In the ring, Randy was a fine boxer with just enough firepower and toughness to take on the best. Outside the ring, Randy was always a true gentleman, a role model to the way fighters should act. A credit to the sport. I always thought of him as the second coming of Gene Tunney. Randy had all the characteristics of Gene: educated, clever gift of gab, plus a college background. Randy was a talented writer, his articles often appearing in major newspapers and magazines.

Randy upset Wepner for that state title but lost it back to Chuck a few months later. I missed their first fight but attended the second and third fights in their fight trilogy, all well-fought encounters. Although hot rivals, they treated each other with deep respect; it was a breath of fresh air for boxing.

After Chuck regained his title in the second Neumann fight, he took on the top-rated Ernie Terrell in Atlantic City. Ernie was a tough man to fight; many fighters avoided him if they possibly could. A very tall, elongated heavyweight with a very long reach and a dartlike jab much like the tongue of a snake, which he used constantly. Ernie was very adept at tying up an opponent, thereby smothering his foe's punching ability. On paper this fight appeared to be another badly cut Chuck Wepner going down to defeat from that very good stinging jab of Ernie's.

The only fighter I ever saw to outjab Ernie was Muhammad Ali in their title bout won by Ali on a 15-round decision. I didn't think Ali could do it, but he certainly did in a battle of left jabs that had Terrell a badly swollen mess at the finish.

Chuck fooled everyone. He not only went the full 12 rounds; he gained the controversial win. Which was OK with me. I was happy Chuck finally got the benefit of the doubt and didn't fall victim to the cuts in a crucial fight. That feat alone was enough indeed to convince the ref and Wepner's fans of the victory.

In 1974 Chuck met Randy Neumann in their third fight, each having won 12-round decisions over each other. The rubber match would be held in Madison Square Garden.

This was Randy's big night; he boxed beautifully. In the seventh round, with Randy ahead, they clashed heads. The cut on Randy's eye was so severe the ref stopped the fight, thereby giving Wepner a TKO win. The "go to the scorecards" rule was not in effect yet. At that time they went by the old standby: "Protect yourself at all times." If a fighter got cut from a head butt, whether intentional or unintentional, his cutman had to keep it under control. If he couldn't and the cut got worse, the ref or doctor could stop the fight, and the fighter lost by TKO.

Garden fans were stunned. It was always *Chuck* who got stopped on cuts—what a turnaround. I believe it was a "first" in Chuck's career. One had to feel sorry for Randy, but that's the fight game. As longtime boxing commentator Larry Merchant always said, "the theater of the unexpected," that's boxing.

Way out west another hot heavyweight prospect was emerging. To Salt Lake City boxing fans, their "cowboy" was destined to become the heavyweight champion of the world. It was time to give him a test against a rated contender. His team decided Chuck Wepner, a fringe contender, was a respectful opponent that Terry Hinke would have a good chance to add to his winning record. They figured Terry's insurance was that Chuck was so prone to facial cuts. Sound familiar? Shades of Joe Bugner, the English hope.

Naturally Chuck would accept, as he would fight anyone, anytime and anyplace. Surprise! Chuck knocks out the "Cowboy" in the 11th round for a very impressive win.

Meanwhile Muhammad Ali was defeating and defending his title over the very best heavies in an era that produced more heavyweight talent than ever before in the history of the sport. Ali ducked no one. He and his manager/trainer Angelo Dundee would seek out the most dangerous. Few people knew much about Earnie Shavers and Ken Norton when Ali announced he had plans to meet them. Howard Cosell, the top commentator, remarked that Ali was starting to "pick softies," proving in reality that Howard, although a good commentator, knew very little about the sport that made him famous. After he milked it dry, he abandoned it and even verbally abused it after the Larry Holmes–Tex Cobb fight, right on the air. He vowed he would never again lower himself to work in or support boxing. The "blowhard" left the sport, and no one especially missed him. I relished his departure. Carmen Basilio saw through him years before when he called Cosell a phony. His words rang true indeed.

Excuse the Cosell excursion away from our hero's story, but your writer's love for the sport at times carries him away in his desire to protect the sport and let the reader know exactly what was going on at the time.

Ali's team decided it was time for "the Greatest" to have a rest from fighting the best and give him a fight he could easily win. This was done because Ali liked to stay busy, stay in the public's eye and earn money at the same time. They would pick an opponent who would supply Ali with a workout, much like a sparring session but still adding to Ali's appeal.

Chuck Wepner was picked. His eight-fight win streak with those wins over Terrell, Neumann and Hinke helped his image as a contender. A contender with whom Ali and team need not worry about the outcome. The fight was signed and sealed.

Ali could enjoy his "rest" in the months preceding the fight, thereby eating the foods he liked and doing the things he liked to do, with a minimum of gym work. He and Dundee were comfortable with the belief that Ali could cut Wepner up at his leisure, bringing a halt to the fight as he pleased.

They forgot one major thing—Chuck Wepner's *will to win*.

For the first time in his rugged career, Chuck went to a country training camp. He put his whole heart and soul into getting into the best shape of his life. Chuck wasn't going in there just for the money, even though he was a very huge underdog. Some fighters in that position would take the money and run, knowing full well they could not beat the "Great One." Not Chuck, he was going to whip Ali and take that precious title. Ali's team and fans laughed at Wepner's words and said he was "dreaming." In the days leading up to the fight, Ali and his crew played the part to the hilt of the great champion giving a shot at his title to the struggling tenth-rated contender. Wepner was supposed to kiss up to them and be extremely grateful for the opportunity given to him.

What happened was Chuck gave Ali all he could handle in a bruising fight. Ali started getting frustrated along about the fifth round, a round Ali thought would be about the time he would send Chuck to the showers. By the ninth round, Ali was not only frustrated but embarrassed that he couldn't dispatch this dogged contender.

Then it happened: a straight right hand driven into Ali's midsection drove the champion to the canvas. The crowd went completely nuts. Ali got up and boxed his way to round's end. He was boiling angry and started calling the ref Tony Perez a dog for not getting on Chuck for rabbit-punching. I believe it was sour grapes because Ali was also using his well-known holding behind an opponent's neck and pulling his foe into a clinch or pulling him off balance to reduce his opponent's fire-power.

The reader can see this foul used to great extent in the Ali-Frazier and Foreman-Ali fight tapes. In both fights the referees begged Ali to stop, but he simply ignored them. Both referees made it a routine to pry Ali's left glove off Frazier and Foreman's neck as they separated them from each clinch. It was useless to keep on warning him, and to disqual-ify him was completely out of the question. These were multi-million-dollar fights. A disqualification would start a riot and discredit the sport. Also, referees seldom gave Ali any trouble. Refereeing an Ali fight was very lucrative, and the door must be left open to further assign-ments.

I noticed Ali starting to use this tactic as far back as his winning fight over Alonzo Johnson. The old cliché of "protect yourself at all times" was in effect, and Ali used it to his advantage. Only boxing purists would call him out on it, for it definitely was illegal. Yet it did not affect his greatness as a fighter nor discredit him to his legion of admirers.

So the ref was being fair in what was good for the goose was good for the gander. He never chastised Chuck for his rabbit punches.

Ali was infuriated with the audacity of this man still in contention here in the 14th round, knocking him down in the eighth, and he just may take it to a decision. Most fighters going into the final round with a definite lead simply take no chances in the last round to avoid a last-minute attempt by his opponent to "pull out" the win with a lucky punch.

Ali was just too pissed for that scenario. He came out with a blind-ing assault in a desperate attempt to kayo Chuck. He finally hurt Chuck in the last minute and fired an avalanche of punches to drive Chuck to the canvas. Chuck valiantly got up at the count of nine, but he could hardly stand up. Ref Perez had no choice but to stop the fight with only 19 seconds left to the final bell. Chuck fought a magnificent fight only to lose by 15th-round TKO. A great display of the lowly underdog's fight-ing heart and desperate will to win.

It spawned the seed for a relatively unknown movie actor to write and create the fictional character Rocky Balboa in a series of films that made Sylvester Stallone a millionaire and a top Hollywood star as well as a household hero.

For Wepner, he too became known worldwide with a calling card of his knockdown of the great Muhammad Ali a collector's item. His popularity and being known as a "tough guy" earned him two lucrative novelty matches with the top Japanese wrestler Inocki in Japan and a New York ballpark encounter with Andre the Giant, then a TV bout with hot prospect Duane Bobick and a fight in South Africa. Chuck lost both fights. He knew it was time for him to ride off into the sunset, but he fought his last fight trying to defend his beloved New Jersey heavyweight title against Scott Frank, an up-and-coming Jerseyite. Chuck lost the 12-round decision, then retired. He didn't want to become a stepping stone and punching bag for youngsters looking to add his name to their winning resumes. Chuck was and still is a credit to boxing.

The Bayonne Bleeder? No. I'd call him the very essence of the Red Badge of Courage.

Freddie "Red" Cochrane

It was very unlikely that "Red" would ever become "welterweight champion of the world," yet he did. On the night of July 29, 1941, Cochrane, a huge underdog, scored a stunning upset at Newark's Ruppert Stadium over kingpin Fritzi Zivic by taking the 15-round decision.

How did he accomplish the upset? Only a few insiders and old-time fight buffs knew the real reason for Zivic's below-par performance.

It's a unique story and a story worth telling, along with Cochrane's rough road to a title match.

Who can forget the movie *Rocky* where Mickey screams at Balboa, "You got to have a *manager*." Of course Mickey becomes both trainer and manager for the Rock on his way to the title.

In the history of boxing, many stories of the managers of the boxers have been written. There have been the legendary managers who went above and beyond to market their fighters and strove diligently to obtain their fighters the most money possible. I like to call them "con men."

Time and time again managers have taken to the ballyhoo and hype to "sell" one of their inferior fighters to promoters for lucrative matches.

Of course it was fairly easy for a manager to move the star of his stable who had great talent. The problem was the ordinary fighters in the stable; it was his job to see they would earn enough coin to sustain a living and also provide the manager a profit. His job was unending. He had to obtain steady work for his charge and also match him correctly to keep his fighter a winning one and stay in the public eye, much like Hollywood actors depend deeply on a good, smart agent to blossom their careers. There also have been over the years many managers who were outright "dogs," leeches who sucked the last drops of blood from their fighters. Hollywood likes to use this type as standard in their boxing movies. A cruel blow to the many honest managers in the fight game.

We focus here on the good ones who were absolutely essential to the sport of boxing, men like Jack "Doc" Kearns, Jack Dempsey's pilot, and Joe Jacobs, Max Schmeling's main man, along with Jack Blackburn, Yank Durham, Angelo Dundee, Lou Duva, Emmanuel Stewart, and Cus D'Amato, to name just a few.

They became world famous, yet none went to business school. Some of the deals they made were on the borderline of business genius. Doc Kearns was noted for actually breaking the banks of Shelby, Montana, by obtaining a super payday for Dempsey in the Gibbons fight.

Willie "the Beard" Gilzenberg was such a manager. He was the pilot of Freddie "Red" Cochrane. How he obtained a shot at the title for Freddie was amazing. Certainly Freddie did nothing to warrant the title opportunity. A title match was the ultimate goal of all fighters, a chance to become world champion. In those glorious days in boxing, the world champion meant everything, like being inaugurated as king.

There were eight weight divisions with one champion in each, except the lightweight division, which for years had an ongoing dispute; the NBA had their champ and the New York Commission had theirs. So only *seven* men could walk the planet and be recognized as world champions.

Today, at last look, I counted 17 weight classes and at least four or more "champs" in each division, plus many "sectional" champs, such as North American, Inter-Continental, etc. Today the world champion is so watered down in means absolutely nothing; every fighter is a champion. I blame this on the money-mad leeches who have infested our sport like fleas on a camel. Sanctioning fees is the name of their game.

Back to Willie Gilzenberg and Cochrane. In no way is it your writer's intention to belittle Red's prowess as a fighter. He was a good fighter in a sea of good fighters who fought each other with zest and zeal in their attempts to gain that shot that was so elusive. Freddie got it because of his wily manager, Gilzenberg, who also got the right location for the fight, his fighter's backyard, which also brought the judge count down from the usual three to only one, as New Jersey used the referee as sole judge. I'm sure Gilzenberg also pushed for a New Jersey ref. Joey Mangold filled the bill.

As lowly challenger, Cochrane would get the short end of the total receipts. Gilly fully knew this, but Gilly not only got his fighter a shot at the crown; he had definite plans of winning that title. The big money would come after Red was champ. Insiders believed Gilly and Red were having pipe dreams and would be lucky if Red could avoid being knocked out.

Your champion was Fritzi Zivic who had recently defended his title with a smoking kayo victory over the immortal "Hammering" Henry Armstrong at MSG. The following true account reads like a Hollywood script.

Gilly knew full well that Freddie "Red" Cochrane could not beat Fritzi Zivic. In order to do so, Red would need tremendous help. Gilly called the Cochrane team together to let them know of the plan he devised. A large bit of skullduggery and mental sparring would be involved. The great Teddy Atlas always claimed boxing was 75 percent mental.

Zivic, after his great win over Armstrong, kept busy as always, fighting seven times and winning six before he would defend against Cochrane in July of 1941.

The fight was signed and sealed for Ruppert Stadium in Newark, New Jersey. Cochrane's hometown was Elizabeth, New Jersey, a few miles down the road from the stadium. It was thought the fight would do better ticketwise if it were held at Ruppert instead of MSG. Garden fans might not go for a Cochrane challenge.

With the location all settled, Gilly and Co. had to do their very best to get Fritzi's mind off the fight. The first thing in their favor was that Fritzi was convinced he was being fed a "soft one." That put him in a relaxing mood. Second was bringing Fritzi to town a week before the fight and installing him in the best Newark hotel. Third, wine and dine him and introduce him to some gorgeous models and showgirls. It was well known by insiders at the time that Fritzi fell for it hook, line and sinker. Even Fritzi's team was taken in by it. They just didn't believe Cochrane was any kind of threat to Zivic. Why worry? By the way, Red Cochrane honed himself to razor-sharp condition. Red knew boxing; he had over 100 fights under his belt. And the tools he had were ready to spring an upset.

Red had lost over 30 fights on his way to this unlikely title opportunity, but 60-odd wins along with those losses made him a very experienced challenger who certainly maintained a bag of tricks along the way.

Gilly's plan was to *destroy Zivic's legs*. We refer again to the movie *Rocky* when Mickey told Balboa to "stay away from that woman of yours weeks before the fight. They destroy fighter's legs." Poor Adrian.

Apparently Gilly's scheme worked. Zivic, an overwhelming favorite, lost the 15-round decision and his championship to the carrot-topped Jerseyite. The referee, also a Jerseyian, was the lone judge, as per state rules. The dice were loaded all against Zivic by one of the sport's all-time "good" managers. Gilly, as Willie Gilzenberg was affectionately known, would play a huge part in the new champion's career.

The first thing he had to do for his new champion was avoid the number-one contender, Sugar Ray Robinson. There was no possible way Red could defeat the great Sugar Ray. Second, he had to get a money fight for Red before the military could draft him, being that the Second World War was on.

He offered Zivic a return bout, which Fritzi and Co. jumped at. They wanted their title back, with also revenge in mind. But Gilly was indeed a sly one; he offered Zivic the return at MSG, but the fight would be a non-title affair. A reluctant Zivic camp okayed the match, figuring at least they could get revenge for that embarrassing loss in New Jersey. The New York return match was an easy win for Zivic. Fritzi's legs were fine that night, and as everyone expected, he walked off with the ten-round decision.

Now, before the commission could force Cochrane to defend his title as the rules called for or strip him of it, Gilly pulled another grand move. He had to put Red and the title on ice, so he told Red to enlist in the U.S. Navy. Red was the first wartime champ to do so. Joe Louis, Gus Lesnevich and Tony Zale followed, either being drafted or by enlistment. It is not clear which.

Gilly was hoping that by war's end Robinson might outgrow the welterweight division. Also Zivic was showing signs of wear. That would be two stumbling blocks out of the way for Red on his return to action.

Freddie "Red" Cochrane was definitely a "Depression era fighter." He started fighting in the early 1930s and tangled through a maze of very hungry local fighters. Jobs were nonexistent at the time, so any guy who thought he was tough donned the leather mitts to try to earn some money. The small fight clubs were abundant, and the competition was fierce. Elizabeth, New Jersey, Red's hometown, was an incubator for these young pros. Bitter feuds and downright animosity developed between these Depression-hungry local fighters.

The Italian section of the city boasted their beloved Orlando brothers, Tony and Frankie, as their best. Red Cochrane was the Irish section's favorite.

Frankie Orlando and Red clashed in a six-rounder and struggled to a highly disputed draw. Younger brother Tony was working Frankie's corner and had to be restrained from getting at Red when the draw was announced. The Orlando brothers insisted that Frankie was robbed of the decision, and to add to it, they claimed Red was fouling the whole six rounds. They demanded a return bout which Red refused to give them. All this created very bad blood between the fighters, with Frankie's request for a return turned down again and again, as if Red enjoyed antagonizing the Orlandos by his refusals. This dislike carried on the rest of their lives, and I believe it affected Cochrane's popularity with many in Jersey boxing.

In May of 1935, Red beat a town favorite in Mickey Greb, winning a six-round decision. Two months later he was in with a tough Mickey Cohen in Nutley, New Jersey. Red flattened Cohen in two rounds.

Cohen, who didn't have the skill to become a success or a money-maker at boxing, gave up his pugilistic ambitions to seek other avenues where he could use his brawn and his love for being villainous to his advantage.

He became a bouncer, then a bodyguard for "mob" members. He then joined the mob as a hit man. He graduated to the West Coast crime family and then to the heights of that organization. He later became the boss of crime on the West Coast and in Las Vegas.

Little did these two prelim boxers on that night of July 17, 1935, know what fate had in store for them. They both became famous. Cochrane for the "good" as welterweight champion of the world, and Mickey Cohen for the "bad" as a nationally known crime boss.

Through the years, boxing has been the foundation for thousands of successful people, fortunately more good than bad.

Now with the war ending and the servicemen returning to civilian life, Red was eager to get back in the harness and earn some money. He had to rid himself of three years of rust. Gilly lined him up for five fights in two weeks in June of 1945. Of course the opponents were of the "can't win" variety in small towns around the country. They were strictly cannon fodder for Red. And Cochrane delivered five knockouts. In two weeks Red had a date in MSG. Gilly had arranged for a big-money fight with the new rage, KO sensation Rocky Graziano. It would be a meaningful fight for the Rock. He could build himself up to the limits with a win over a world champion. For Red it was finally a chance to make a champion's purse, which was void to him the last three years. Even if he lost he would still be champ. Rocky was a middleweight; Cochrane's title would not be on the line.

The fight was a sensation. Cochrane boxed beautifully, making Rocky swing like a gate. He won the first eight rounds, making Rocky furious and desperate. The Rock finally caught Red with one of his bombs in the ninth round and floored him; the bell came to Red's rescue. Rocky came out for the tenth and final round knowing he had to finish Red or lose a decision. Like a man gone completely berserk, Rocky unloaded everything he had and flattened Red Cochrane to win by a tenth-round kayo.

Needless to say, *Ring* magazine named it the fight of the year for 1945. I believe Red fought the greatest fight of his life, and Rocky was being called the second Stanley Ketchel. Less than two months later they would do it again at the Garden.

Cochrane's great fight against Rocky helped his image somewhat, but a lot of fans, especially Sugar Ray Robinson's, believed he should have defended his title against the long number-one contender who was now called the uncrowned welterweight champion, Sugar Ray. But Gilly and Red's idea was to put Ray off as long as possible so they could cash in on their title. Who really could blame them? A Robinson fight would be Cochrane's finish. So Robinson had to wait, and wait, and *wait*.

The second Graziano vs. Cochrane fight packed the Garden. Only this time Rocky met a totally burned-out fighter. Cochrane left everything he had in their first fight. Red took a fearful beating, floored again and again, but desperately struggling to his feet in a valiant attempt to finish. Again in the tenth and final round, Red's body could not take anymore. He was counted out, Rocky again a tenth-round kayo winner.

By now the heavy pressure was on the commission to get Robinson his title shot. Cochrane had to defend the title or lose it.

Somehow Willie Gilzenberg talked the commission into a Marty

Servo fight with the winner to guarantee a fight with Robinson. Sugar Ray would wait and wait. The sly fox Gilly had Servo accept training expenses, if that, as his share. Servo's team agreed, knowing full well Red was shot, totally shopworn. All they wanted was that precious title. Servo knew he couldn't lose. So five months after his beating by Graziano, Cochrane was again in the Garden ring. It was a mismatch. Cochrane was blown out of there in four rounds. I believe Gilly ducked Robinson again on this one only because Gilly figured Servo would give Red a beating much less than Robinson would. A bit of compassion on Gilly's part. Red Cochrane never fought again.

Your writer always prefers to write about fighters that I have seen perform in the "flesh." I never saw Red fight, although I heard his fights with Graziano and Servo on the *Gillette Cavalcade of Sports* on the radio, narrated by the legendary Bill Corum and Don Dunphy. Dunphy did the blow-by-blow accounts.

That is why 25 years later when I first met Red, I did not immediately recognize him. He was of course one of two champions spawned in Elizabeth, New Jersey, quite an honor for my hometown. Yet Red never really got the hometown superhero adulation he truly deserved.

I believe the bad taste in the mouths of a lot of fans was still lingering from the blood feud with their beloved Orlando Brothers, two of the finest gentlemen boxing ever knew. Red also had a bad score with fans statewide for his inability to defeat "the Garfield Gunner" Tippy Larkin, who defeated Cochrane *five times*, all by decision. Try as he might, Red could never beat Tippy, a New Jersey favorite. Many fans felt that if anyone should be champion it should be Larkin.

No fault of Red, he simply fought who they put in front of him. Another drawback for Red was that he never fought on national TV. His career ended before boxing went to television big time.

Being champion was enough to be known nationally. Yet his face was not.

Ring magazine reported through the years of a rash of Cochrane impersonators. Con men were using his name to hustle drinks and loans and business deals with unsuspecting boxing lovers.

When Red left the ring, he opened a bar and grill here in New Jersey which proved successful. He never made that "comeback" that so many fighters do, only to have their hopes shattered.

The night I met Red a small incident happened which I call "the five dollar bill episode." Some may think the story trivial, but I think it's worth telling. A life's lesson, perhaps.

A friend and I went to the Elizabeth Elks Club to see a Golden Gloves card. The fights were hot and heavy when midway an intermission was called so the club could make some money at their bar. My friend and I hustled to the bar which was soon packed, men standing three and four deep waiting to be served. The man next to me was visibly upset; he claimed he had given a five dollar bill for his beer and only received coins for change of a dollar. The crowd and the size of the bartender was enough to keep this very upset man in control of any angry outburst, and he timidly requested the barkeep to check the cash register to see if a five was mixed in with the one dollar bills.

The bartender sarcastically refused as he tried to keep from being overwhelmed by those waiting for their drinks during this 15-minute break. Five dollars meant a lot in those days to hardworking people. The man continued to complain. His words fell on deaf ears as far as the barkeep was concerned.

On my left next to my friend was a small red-headed man with tough-looking facial features. He barked at the bartender, calling him over. The barman came over immediately in a quick change of his earlier attitude. The redhead in a much lowered voice said, "Ed, cut the crap. Give the guy a break and give him his proper change. Now."

The barkeep quickly pulled four one dollar bills from the register and placed them in front of the complainant. What a complete turnaround, I thought. Who was that guy? Probably the boss of the Elks Club. How else could he gain so much respect?

After asking a few questions, I found out the redhead was none other than Freddie "Red" Cochrane, the former welterweight champion of the world. Of course the bartender agreed with Red; he had no desire to tangle with the former champion.

The intermission was over and the fights had started again. As we walked back to our seats, I caught up with Red and introduced myself. We spoke for about a minute. I found him to be very cordial and polite. I sat down to resume watching the fights. I watched, but nothing registered. I couldn't stop thinking about Red Cochrane. For years I had heard stories of his character as an obnoxious, cocky wise guy whom I developed a dislike for.

His actions that night were not consistent with such a character. Tonight he showed compassion and concern for a fight fan he didn't even know. He showed class and acted like a champion in our short conversation. *He changed my mind.* I thought back to his first Graziano fight, ahead all the way only to be stopped in that fateful last round. In the return, down many times, he desperately tried to finish, but flesh and blood can only take so much, and again he only lost by kayo. I also believe Red fell victim to Cochrane "bashers" over the years. One thing's for sure, Freddie Red Cochrane was no quitter. Like him or dislike him, one had to accept Freddie for what he was: an honest workman who did what he had to in order to gain the championship, which every fighter dreamed of and sacrificed for. If a little mental strategy was needed to obtain that goal, so be it.

Muhammad Ali was a master at playing head games with his opponents as he prepared them for the fight. Most of his foes couldn't compete against Ali's onslaught of words and actions, from the time the fight was signed to the weigh-in and the opening bell. He even taunted them during the fight. Ali diverted 50 percent of his opponents' strategy and game plan off the fight and onto his outrageous antics. Ali was brilliant at it.

I recall way before Ali's time a light heavy champ, Melio Bettina, who had a manager who claimed to be a magician and hypnotist; his name was Jimmy Grippo. He tried to hypnotize and put the hex on Melio's opponents. It never worked, but it made for good copy anyway.

Ali's way was much better, and it always worked. And so did Willie Gilzenberg's method.

Rocky Graziano:
The Dead End Kid

It's almost impossible to omit Rocky Graziano from writings about New Jersey boxing. A product of the Lower East Side of New York City, this "Happy Hoodlum" spent half of his first 20 years in boys' reform schools, an incorrigible punk who was ignorant of the meaning of the word "discipline" or orderly conduct. His own father called him the "devil." He made his mother's life a living hell. She tried desperately to keep him out of jail and teach him to respect the law. All in vain.

Rocky's only answer to anyone of authority who took him to task for his lawlessness was a smashing right-hand punch to his antagonist's jaw, rendering that person unconscious. God did grace Rocky with a tremendous punch and a very muscular body.

Some of Rocky's thug friends became professional boxers and kept after Rocky to start boxing, claiming the Rock was a natural and could make some coin doing what he was already doing for nothing on the streets, knocking people out.

Rocky saw that these friends of his always had some money. Rocky wanted some of that bread too and started boxing amateur. He did well and hocked the watches a winner receives.

For the first time in his life he earned some honest money. He wanted more, so he turned pro.

Little did he know that this was the beginning of the most remarkable run of a boxer or any athlete in sports history to battle his way up from rags and unbelievable despair to riches and notoriety the world over. His name became a household word and he a multimillionaire. He eventually became America's "Goombah," loved by all. His transformation from evil to beloved started with his first pro fights. It blossomed the length of his boxing career and after.

Those first pro fights took place in my hometown, Elizabeth, New Jersey, in a tiny fight club known as Scott Hall in the heart of the city. Rocky scored a one-round knockout over Gilbert Vasquez, a local pug who later became a shoemaker and had a store on the corner of Cherry Street and Rahway Avenue next to the railroad bridge. When Rocky became famous, Vasquez never stopped telling his customers of his one-round "battle" with the Rock.

Graziano fought a number of times at Scott Hall, always in the preliminaries, four- and six-round fights, gaining needed experience. He finally knocked out a promising and popular local boy, Joe Curcio. Curcio would become a New Jersey favorite in the years ahead, headlining cards all over the state. So it was on to New York for Rocky with the Curcio win. It is ironic that Clint Miller, a top featherweight at the time and Elizabeth's pride, saw Rocky's fights at Scott Hall and predicted that this wild-swinging slugger would someday become middleweight champion of the world. Rocky couldn't box and had no defense, only that sledgehammer right. Everyone said Clint must have become punchy. They believed any fighter with a little boxing knowledge would make short work of this wild man. But Clint insisted he was right. He must have seen the tremendous power Rocky possessed. If Rocky could build around that power, he could do it. An extremely far-fetched prediction, yet Clint Miller always stood by it.

Rocky did very little training for these prelim fights. He simply told his trainer, sign them up and I'll knock 'em out.

But even Rocky knew that you can't knock everyone out, and as the opposition got better, the fights would go longer and even to decisions. If he wanted to keep making money, he had to get himself in shape to go the rounds and win.

He even got himself a top manager in Irving Cohen, a man that could move a fighter. Irving immediately got Whitey Bimstein to train the Rock.

Rocky was soon fighting in the very tough New York club circuit, mostly winning but sometimes losing to slick boxers. Rocky hated any fighter who could move and stick out that jab and avoid being hit. It would drive the Rock crazy.

The fans loved Rocky's style, which was seek and destroy. He constantly moved in on his opponent, throwing that booming right hand, and every time he threw it, which was often, the crowd would roar, whether it landed or not.

One fighter who drove Rocky completely nuts was Steve Riggio; he won two six-round decisions over Rocky by jabbing and running for dear life. Rocky couldn't understand how the judges could possibly give Riggio the nod. In their second fight, Rocky threw the usual amount of right hands but never connected. Rocky was so upset and angry his handlers had to hold him back from knocking down Riggio's dressing room door and attacking him.

Rock also lost twice to rough, tough Harold Green who stood right in the pocket with Rocky, took some of Rocky's best shots, and retaliated with his own. Green had more experience and better defense, which Rocky still lacked. Green deserved the wins, and Rocky learned from it. It proved to him that in order to be on top, you must develop some kind of defense. Rocky started to really take his training seriously, and became a better fighter for it.

Things were shaping up for Rocky with his boxing career. But all at once the bottom fell out. Rocky got drafted into the Army. Rocky knew exactly nothing of the Army. He only knew the dog-eat-dog way of life on New York's East Side and his survival of the many harsh years he spent in New York's toughest reform schools. Once in the Army, Rocky would not listen to any of his NCOs' orders. He slept in in the mornings and wouldn't go with his company on their daily drills. Needless to say, he was taken by the MPs to stand before the company commander.

Rocky explained to the officer he did not understand all this crap of marching, drilling and lectures. He told the CO, "Give me a gun and send me to the war." The officer started to tongue lash the Rock, who promptly flattened the CO and went AWOL, running away to his beloved buddies on the Lower East Side.

He was picked up a few days later by the Army and made to stand court-martial. He was convicted and sent to the Army prison at Fort Levenworth.

After serving his time, Rocky returned to New York and resumed his career.

Around this time Rocky met the love of his life, a Jewish-American girl named Norma. She is the one who finally tamed this wild stallion. She roped him, broke him and put him on a straight and narrow path to the beloved hero he eventually became.

Rocky put his all in on his training and his fights. A couple more kayo wins got him a fight in Madison Square Garden against a huge winning kayo artist the Garden was grooming for big major fights. Rocky would be cannon fodder for vicious punching Billy Arnold out of Philadelphia.

The first-round bell rang, and Arnold smashed Rocky all over the ring. Rocky was lucky to finish the round. The beating continued on until the third round when Rocky in desperation went berserk with an all-out attack, throwing right-hand bombs from all angles, putting Arnold down for the knockout win. Rocky, a 10–1 underdog, became an overnight sensation. Five more smashing knockout wins at the Garden and Rocky was the darling of New York and New Jersey boxing f ans who packed the Garden each time. He kayoed New Jersey's welterweight champion of the world, Freddie "Red" Cochrane, *twice*. In their first fight Rocky had to pull it out in the final round with a blazing kayo—he was behind on the scorecards. His right-hand knockout wallop became legendary. He is the only fighter I ever remember that each time he threw the right hand the crowd would roar, and he threw it often.

His work at MSG came to its climax. He was matched with middleweight champion Tony Zale at Yankee Stadium. Zale had served three and a half years in the Navy. On his release he was looking for a huge payday with a popular challenger. He certainly had one waiting—Mike Jacobs' million-dollar baby Rocky Graziano.

Their fight was a blood-spattered classic. Both fighters hit the canvas in a back-and-forth brawl. Rocky was finally knocked out from a vicious left hook to the body by Zale. That fight is still talked and written about to this day.

The return match was fought in Chicago and was another splendid effort by both warriors, with a bloody Rocky making a last-ditch, all-out effort to kayo Zale. The end came in the sixth round, same as their first fight. Rocky finally made it; he was now the undisputed middleweight champion of the world.

Rocky defended his title against Zale at Ruppert Stadium, Newark, New Jersey, on June 10, 1948, with yours truly in attendance. It only lasted three rounds, with Zale punching Rocky with huge shots all the way. Rocky was floored in the third and got up very wobbly. A faint-hearted referee would have stopped it right then. But Paul Cavaleir, the ref, believed a champion should be given every opportunity to keep his championship. He wiped off the Rock's gloves, and then Rocky threw a left jab at the oncoming Zale, who fired his well-known left hook to Rocky's jaw. It looked like that left would decapitate the Rock; he went down flat on his back. His legs never left the position they were in. It proved Rocky was out cold before he hit the canvas. When he did hit the canvas, his legs popped out straight in the full prone position. The ref counted the full ten count and Rocky never moved. It was one of the most brutal knockouts I have ever seen. Fighters have been known to have their legs broken with such a knockdown.

The Zale-Graziano trilogy is well known in boxing lore. Rocky was still very popular. He fought on.

His autobiography was a best seller. The New York News printed a part of the story each day and made a fortune on it. Hollywood turned out the film *Somebody Up There Likes Me*, the same as the book. Paul Newman became a star portraying the Rock. Perry Como sang the picture's song, also called "Somebody Up There Likes Me."

After the third Zale fight, Rocky had two major bouts. He knocked out New Jersey Golden Boy Charley Fusari in New York's Polo Grounds. Again Rocky had to pull it out in the tenth and final round with his right-hand bombs. Fusari was ahead on all cards. The fans adored him for these great come-from-behind wins.

And finally the fight everyone wanted to see for years: a Sugar Ray Robinson vs. Rocky Graziano title bout. Robby was now champ, having defeated Jake LaMotta for the crown. Rocky went undefeated in 21 fights after losing to Zale, 17 by knockout. Everyone knew the Rock couldn't beat Robby but they also knew it would be a great fight, and there was always the Rock's great right-hand wallop for an upset.

They fought on April 16, 1952, at Chicago Stadium. It was over in three rounds; the great Sugar Ray Robinson knocked out Rocky, but not before picking himself up off the deck from one of them Rocky right-hand bombs.

Graziano lost his next fight on decision to the undefeated Chuck Davey and then retired.

Rocky became an instant TV commercial star. He made many. Every company was after him. Rocky claimed he made more money doing commercials than he made in his entire ring career.

Martha Raye hired the Rock to be her boyfriend on her TV show; he was her beloved "Goombah." Rocky became quite the comedian and started appearing on all the TV shows as a guest. The money was rolling in for him, but Norma had to put him on an allowance. If she didn't, he would have spent it all. He spent money like a drunken sailor. She watched the bread, and Rocky lived out his life a millionaire. Happy going for a dead-end kid.

Rocky was a huge player in Jersey boxing. He fought some of his prelims in my hometown. He kayoed Jersey fighters Joe Curcio twice, Red Cochrane twice and our Golden Boy Charley Fusari. For his big fights he trained in Summit, New Jersey, at the old Madame Bay training camp. He lost his title at Newark, and Jersey fans loved him for his big punch. And I was one of them.

Promoter George "Korn" Kobb

This man was responsible for bringing boxing on a large scale to Elizabeth, New Jersey. He started out running shows at tiny Scott Hall in the heart of the city. He used local prelim fighters, and the main event was usually a six-rounder. He'd never get rich at it because the seating in the hall was sparse.

George was the announcer, promoter, ticket seller, matchmaker and all-around man at his shows. His matchmaking was terrific, all good, hard-fought fights that sold out the hall weekly.

From his success at Scott he graduated to the Elizabeth Armory, where he started to bring in big names such as Willie Pep, Fritzi Zivic, Freddie Archer, Tippy Larkin, Beau Jack and the great Sugar Ray Robinson, just to name a few. Robby came to town three times, all KO wins. Yet the Armory became known as the "House of Upsets" after some of the big names got knocked off. Again it was all credited to Kobb's smart matchmaking.

The Armory ran all winter; then in the spring and summer Kobb ran his shows at the Twin City Bowl, an open-air arena on the Newark-Elizabeth city line.

As a youngster I attended both locations. After an Armory show, one had to go home and put all the clothes worn that night in the hamper for washing and take a shower to get the stink of cigarette and cigar smoke off your body, then shampoo your hair which would reek with smoke odor.

It was winter, and the Armory was closed up tight, with no exhaust fans. I couldn't believe how thick the smoke was; you could cut it with a knife. The nonsmoking fans suffered, but it was worth it—the fights were great. The open-air fights at Twin City Bowl were okay, but you always had the threat of rain and postponement.

To this 14-year-old, George Kobb was a saint. He allowed me to see all my big-name heroes in the flesh. Before Kobb, I only heard them on radio, blow by blow with Don Dunphy and Bill Corumn, with Gillette Blue Blades as sponsor.

It's strange how a kid thinks. I had a few amateur fights at the Armory, and I was in awe of George "Korn" Kobb as he introduced me to the crowd. After hearing him announce all those great fighters over the past years, to me it was a great honor having him announce me. I was very proud of myself.

George did well with his promotions until TV flooded the airways with fights six days a week. People could see the fights for free. Kobb's promotions slowed down to a few fights a year; then he threw in the towel. Jersey boxing was in the doldrums. It stayed that way until the Atlantic City casinos opened up. The owners found that staging fights was a great way to get the gamblers in. They could gamble before and after the fights; all the casinos used boxing to enhance their business. It worked out fine for years.

All old-timers remember George "Korn" Kobb; he simply was the best.

Please Don't Pass the Sugar: Sugar Ray Robinson

He was tall for a lightweight, very rangy, with those supple muscles and slope shoulders that come with terrific punchers. He could box brilliantly, and if need be, set down and trade bombs with the best punchers in three weight divisions. In short, he could outbox the boxers, outslug the sluggers and even outbolo the bolo punchers. He also was the possessor of an iron jaw, having never been stopped in well over 200 fights. Only once did he fail to finish, and that was due to heat in a bout where the referee had to be replaced because of heatstroke. With all the fine qualities plus the iron jaw, Sugar Ray Robinson seemed destined to become a boxing legend. And he did.

In my 65 years of watching the fights, I have never seen his like. He was the greatest. And he knew it. He had a hell of an ego. He started as a pro at the end of the 1930s and tore through a maze of great fighters on his way to immortality. The boxing writers quickly nicknamed him "Sugar," for he was sweet as sugar. Thus you had "Sugar Ray Robinson." The words *flawless*, *superb*, *impeccable*, and *class* were synonymous with Ray, and he lived it and enjoyed it.

Outside the ring he was the Beau Brommell of boxing. He dressed like a prince and drove a flaming pink Caddy convertible. While fighting in Europe, the British press called him his "sugarship"—the Toast of Great Britain, and the world.

When the welterweight title was up for grabs after Marty Servo's forced retirement, a tournament was suggested, pitting the top-ten welters to fight it out for the vacant crown. Only one man stepped forward to oppose the great Sugar. That man was Tommy Bell. Hell, the other welters knew they had no chance, Sugar had beaten Servo two times before he had won the title and had also beaten Bell before. But Bell was determined and hungry. A shot at the title and a payday he couldn't refuse.

Bell, a good fighter, fought the fight of his life that night and even managed to put Robby on the deck. Sugar came back to floor Bell and win the 15-round decision and the championship in a rousing fight. One reporter wrote, "He, Sugar Ray, manages to look classy even while on the canvas."

Sugar Ray was finally champ. Along came the copycats. Any fighter who had a fairly smooth boxing style called himself "Sugar." Preliminary fighters who were black and had Ray for a first name were automatically "Sugar Ray." It was simply this: in boxing, the word "Sugar" meant *great*.

Robinson never said it, but he resented anyone using his nickname. But I believe most fans knew it. Even before Robby won the title, George Costner, a fighter who many were saying was another Sugar Ray, started demanding a match with Robinson. He was smooth and he could fight. The news media started billing him as George "Sugar" Costner. Little did they know that doing just that would be George's ruination.

Robinson gave Costner the fight he was clamoring for; result—the headlines read, "Sugar Ray Kayos Sugar George in One." Costner was flattened like a pancake. One could hear Ray say, "How dare he use my nickname." There is only one Sugar Ray.

Costner still wasn't satisfied. He went on a win streak and kept hollering for a return match. After all, Costner had a great ledger; he had 73 wins with only a handful of losses. Sugar Ray figured he better put an end to this Sugar George bit once and for all. So, after five years, they met again—and one more time George was "KOed in One." I think Ray got the final word out: "Don't mess with my Sugar." Ray's ego was satisfied.

Costner went on to win three fights after his Robinson loss, winning in ten over the then-current lightweight champion, Ike Williams, then defeating the future welterweight champ, Kid Gavilan. Two great Hall of Famers. That's how good Costner was. In his next fight, also a winning one, he found out he had a detached retina. Doctors told him if he continued to fight, he would go blind. Costner did quit, still at the top of his form. The sad thing is he did go blind later in life. He was a damn good fighter, leaving a 77–10–5 record with 48 kayos. Today's fighters are lucky to fight 40 times in an entire career, never mind 48 kayos. If Costner were around today, he would be a superstar. He made the mistake of being called "Sugar," and we all know there was only one Sugar—and his name was Ray Robinson.

Till this day the beat goes on, with the Leonards, Mosleys, etc. "Sugar" in boxing means *great* and also *winner*. And everyone wants to be a winner.

The Great Sugar Ray

It's appropriate near the finale of my boxing stories to write about the greatest fighter I have ever seen in my 75-year love affair with the sport of boxing.

He had a rule that he followed to the letter. He would not fight if he wasn't 100 percent physically or mentally fit. All conditions had to be a go. Naturally the money, the ref, the size of the ring, trunk colors, etc., were only a few reasons he might balk. In short he was a pain in the ass to promoters, yet in a way it might have been a bonus for the fans. They knew when he entered the ring he was at his very best. If he lost, there was never an excuse.

Walker Smith was his name. Boxing fans knew him as "Sugar Ray" Robinson. He picked up the "Sugar" from boxing writers of the day who called his style sweet, hence "Sugar." The "Harlem Daddy," a legend in his own time. In over 200 fights he was never kayoed. He failed to answer the final bell only once when on a brutally hot night in Yankee Stadium, fighting for Joey Maxim's light heavyweight title and spotting Joey 16 pounds, Robby succumbed to heatstroke while a mile ahead on all three cards at the end of the 13th round. The heat kayoed referee Ruby Goldstein in the tenth, and he was replaced by Ray Miller. It was 104 degrees in the stadium, and only God knows how much under the ring lights.

While Maxim laid back, Robby was doing all the fighting. His aggression was his downfall. He could not get off his stool for the 14th round, thus enabling Maxim to retain his title with a TKO win.

Sugar's performance that night proved to any skeptics just what a ring marvel he was. His will to win would never be questioned. The Sugarman was a flawless boxer, a great puncher; his ring smarts were beyond

164

belief. His jaw was like iron. He mastered every trait a fighter should have: jab, cross, hook, uppercut, feints, counterpunching, stamina, heart, chin, footwork, and condition. Seldom cut or floored, he had great defense and outstanding offense.

Once while fighting Kid Gavilan, the great bolo puncher, he showed the kid the proper way to throw that difficult punch. He out boloed the Kid, beating Gavilan *twice*.

In December of 1947, Sugar signed for a non-title fight in the Armory of my hometown, Elizabeth, New Jersey. He was the undisputed welterweight champion of the world.

As soon as your writer heard the news, I started saving my pennies to purchase a balcony seat at the "staggering" cost of $1.50. The days couldn't pass fast enough as I waited patiently. On the night of the fight, I hotfooted it down to the Armory. To a 13-year-old boy who loved boxing, it indeed was a great day.

As you approached the big drill shed, you couldn't miss this huge flamingo-pink Cadillac parked in front of the main door. One of Sugar's entourage was on guard watching as the crowd gawked at this beautiful Caddy, making sure there weren't any souvenir hunters in the crowd. On the doors on each side of the car was in very fancy print the name "Sugar Ray Robinson, Champion."

The guard I mentioned was one of Sugar's so-called entourage, a group of hangers-on who preyed on Sugar throughout his career. Professional "leeches" who at the end abandoned Sugar.

His opponent for this fight would be Billy Nixon, a Philly fighter who had a good resume. He had scored many good wins in main events in Philly and New York rings. Experienced, he had 38 fights and only lost a handful against good competition. But let's face it, he was a kiddy car going up against the big pink Caddy.

My balcony seat was a perfect view of the ring. After enjoying the prelims I was in awe of the Great One making his way to the ring. He had his familiar white robe with the white towel around his neck. The crowd was buzzing. It was a scene I will remember for the rest of my life. I would see literally thousands of fights after this night, yet I never saw a fighter enter the ring as Sugar Ray did that night.

Slick and cool with confidence above and beyond normal human beings. He slipped through the ropes and danced around the ring.

He gave the impression that he and he alone owned that ring; it was his throne room and he was king. This was his domain, his place in life, and no one dared threaten him. The referee and his opponent were merely tools he would use to showcase his skills to his fans. When he thought they had their money's worth, he would simply dispatch his opponent. Nixon went out in six. Body punches that could be heard up in the balcony did him in.

As Sugar waited for the official announcement, he took a comb out of his robe pocket and made sure he had every hair on his head in place.

That my dear reader is the impression Sugar Ray gave to a young boy seeing him "live" for the first time. That boy went home that night and dreamed the impossible dream that he too could become a fighter of Sugar Ray's caliber.

Yet this welterweight champion was not a role model. Many people despised him, especially some promoters he antagonized over the years with sometimes trivial matters. He always acted aloof and had a conceited attitude. His character left much to be desired. But as a professional boxer, he was simply the very best. He was truly magnificent. One of a kind.

The Nixon fight was Sugar's third visit to our city, all kayo wins. In those days, fighters had to fight often, even world champions, to make a buck. The champions needed those non-title bouts, which they engaged in frequently to enhance their yearly income. By fighting so often, fighters honed their skills and learned their craft well. Club fighters could actually make a decent living then because of the many clubs around the country. The metropolitan area was indeed a hotbed of boxing. That's why so many top contenders developed there.

Sugar Ray turned pro at Madison Square Garden in New York City on October 4, 1940, in a prelim on the Armstrong-Zivic welterweight championship card. Sugar scored a first-round kayo win. The great Henry Armstrong wasn't that fortunate; he lost his title to Zivic in the main event.

It is said that Sugar, brokenhearted that his idol lost, broke into Armstrong's dressing room and, seeing Henry sitting on a rundown table nursing his badly swollen face, cried out to him, "Henry I'll get that guy for you." Armstrong in amazement mumbled, "who the hell is this kid?" through badly swollen lips. An Armstrong handler told him that the young punk had scored a one-round kayo in his pro debut earlier that evening and was "feeling his oats."

Exactly one year and a few weeks later in the same arena and now sporting an undefeated record of 25–0 with 20 knockouts, the "punk kid" got even for Armstrong by defeating Fritzi Zivic, the former champion, in ten rounds. Zivic had recently lost his title in a huge upset to Freddie "Red" Cochrane, who enlisted in the Navy and thereby put the title on ice for four years.

Sugar put frosting on the first Zivic win by stopping Fritzi two and a half months later in the tenth round, thereby cementing his claim of "getting that guy" for Armstrong.

By now everyone was calling Sugar the uncrowned welterweight champion. It would remain that way until after World War II.

The commissions decided to stage a tournament of welterweight contenders, with the winner to become champion. Any top-ten welterweight was eligible. Only one fighter stepped forward to compete against Sugar Ray, that being Tommy Bell, a very good fighter from Youngstown, Ohio. He had lost a decision to Sugar a year earlier. But first Sugar had a fight scheduled with a tough middleweight in Cleveland, Ohio.

Your writer has always been baffled with why this fight with Artie Levine was rarely mentioned by fans of the day or boxing historians of the present, or even hard-core Sugar Ray fans of today who collect Robinson memorabilia and stories of their hero. Did everyone miss it?

It is my belief that the Levine fight was Sugar Ray's greatest ever. It tested him down to the bone. Sugar is remembered for his great battles, with LaMotta, Zivic, Basilio, Gavilan, Turpin, Fullmer, etc. They were classics, yet to me the least mentioned was his very best.

Sugar Ray took the fight just six weeks before he would end his five-year wait to challenge for the world welterweight title against Tommy Bell at Madison Square Garden, New York City.

As always, Sugar went in with all systems go. The only concession he gave up was 9¼ pounds to Levine. Sugar weighed 150 pounds to Artie's 159¼. Sugar was used to fighting middleweights, so it didn't faze him. But just maybe he failed to size up Levine properly. I wonder if Sugar and his team knew that Artie Levine was one tough hombre. A former Marine of a rough background, the ruggedly handsome puncher had a resume of over 40 fights, losing very few and with a huge kayo average. At 21 years of age, he was very young and extremely hungry. Both were at their peak; Sugar was 25 years old.

Another item George Gainford, Sugar's pilot, missed is the caliber of opponents Levine had been mixing with. He started as a pro at age 16 and never had a soft touch like so many fighters do in their early development. Levine was never knocked out before. Maybe the fight should have been held at MSG. At the time it was the deluxe showcase of boxing. Cleveland was a good fight town, but it didn't offer the publicity of the Garden. It's not known if radio or just how many newspapers sent reporters to cover the fight. Certainly not near as many as if the fight was held at MSG. These are the only reasons the fight left little for boxing fans to remember.

Sugar would receive $12,500, a good sum for an uncrowned champion in that time.

Sugar Ray entered that Cleveland ring with all his usual self-confidence. He engaged the youthful upstart, whom he didn't have to look for. Levine was right there. Going into the fourth round, little did Sugar know that this would be his greatest fight, one in which he had to call on all his resolve to win. Midway through the round, a terrific left hook followed by a booming right put the Great One on his back. All hell broke loose in the arena as Sugar struggled to beat the count. He barely made it upright at nine and was in deep distress. Only his experience and skill enabled him to last out the round, and with Levine's lack of finishing knowledge, the youngster blew it big time, all to Sugar's advantage. Robinson would later admit he did not remember fighting the fifth and sixth rounds. He claimed to have "woken up" in the seventh round. He was on "automatic pilot" the two previous rounds. Again proof of a great fighter.

Levine was landing his right hand often, a punch Sugar had easily avoided in all his fights up till then. It shows just how hurt he was. Sugar started going to Levine's body and boxing like never before to survive.

Sugar had won the first three rounds, but lost the middle rounds while recovering from that brutal knockdown. He knew he had to box smartly to gain the decision over the crude puncher.

Sugar was desperate going into the tenth and final round. He didn't want to go to the scorecards. That emphatic knockdown along with the many right hands he caught that night could spell defeat for him.

The body punches were paying off for Sugar Ray. It had slowed down Levine's punches, and midway in the tenth, Sugar caught Levine with a blazing right hand to the body. Sugar cornered Levine and cut loose with a barrage only Sugar could throw. An avalanche of accurate punches to the head and body drove Levine to the canvas. He was counted out for the first time in his career of over 40 fights. Sugar got rid of his antagonist, the hell-bent-for-leather former Marine. This was the closest Sugar ever came to being kayoed in 200 fights.

Robinson, who seldom gave any credit to his opponents, in later years, while knocking his manager-trainer, George Gainford, said, "former heavyweight champion Floyd Patterson's manager, Gus D'Amato, gets Floyd a $100,000 purse to defend against a fighter making his pro debut, Pete Rademacher. George Gainford gets me $12,500 for Artie Levine." To your writer, that speaks volumes for Artie Levine. Unknowingly, Sugar gave praise to one of his opponents.

What the hell happened? It was hard for fans to believe. Robby had to pull out all the stops and struggle feverishly for the victory over a fringe 160-pound contender whose walk-in style was made for Sugar. And why was Sugar getting caught with the lead right hands? Was Sugar overconfident? Was Sugar ill or did he have an off night? Was Artie Levine that good? There were so many questions the fans needed answered.

As stated earlier, Robby never entered a ring unprepared. Your writer believes the solid knockdown put Sugar off his stride and rhythm. He was hurt badly and had to slowly regain his mode of fighting. He was fortunate that his very youthful opponent was a poor finisher. God forbid if that was a Fritzi Zivic in there that night. Another factor is Levine was a very good banger. That's probably why he never got a return with the Sugarman. Robinson with this fight, his greatest, proved just how great he was. The fight for Levine gained him two main events in MSG. Later on Levine and Robinson's names would entwine once more.

Levine would fight another Jewish-American in a very rare main event where both headliners were Jewish. Artie was only partial Jewish, but the fans flocked to see Artie outpoint the popular Herbie Kronowitz in a spirited ten-rounder.

The promoter decided to throw Artie against the power-hitting "Black Jack" Billy Fox. Fox had kayoed all his opponents but one. Thirty-seven KO wins with one knockout loss. Two real bangers should supply a terrific fight.

Levine went toe to toe with Billy Fox; they slammed away at each other the entire first round. In the second, Artie had Fox out on his feet, staggering around the ring. But again, as in the Sugar Ray fight, Artie failed to finish his heavier foe. Fox barely lasted the round and came out with blood in his eye in the third. They exchanged furiously until Fox's power overwhelmed the brave Levine. Artie was dropped and the ref halted the bout.

Levine took a year off and then made his comeback. He fought another two years and retired. He was a burned-out fighter at age 24. He started at an early age and was through at an early age. Many fighters of that era did the same. Tony Janiro and Tami Mauriello come to mind; both finished at 25.

As for Sugar Ray, six weeks after his battle with Levine and after a wait of five years, he got his shot at the title.

Tommy Bell fought the fight of his life against Robby, even flooring the Great One along the way. Sugar evened the score by dropping Bell in round 11 and taking the unanimous 15-round decision and that elusive welterweight crown. Sugar Ray finally got what he so desperately wanted, championship of the 147-pounders. His prize turned out to be a hollow shell for Sugar, to his dismay. In his five-year wait, he played hell with the top-ten welters; then with hardly any competition left for him, he still had to fight middleweights. Another problem he now had as king was making the 147-pound weight limit.

His team scoured the welter top-ten for a willing opponent to offer him a title shot. They came up with Jimmy Doyle, a West Coast fighter, a very good boxer but with little power. Doyle was hungry and willing. Jimmy was 22 years old. The Robinson fight would be his last. This was another fight of Sugar's that seemed to fall through the cracks. It is seldom mentioned by boxing writers, boxing historians or Sugar Ray buffs, much like the Sugar vs. Levine fight, both held in Cleveland, Ohio.

Doyle had fought Levine a year before and had the much stronger and heavier Levine in a neat bloody package going into the ninth round. The roof fell in on Jimmy when Artie finally connected with his big guns. Doyle took a brutal beating, going down three times. He was unconscious when taken to the hospital by stretcher. He was diagnosed as having a severe brain concussion, given bed rest and released. Under today's standards with all-out elite X-rays and scans, it is doubtful that Doyle would have gotten permission to fight again. But that was then, and this is now. Doyle could have had a brain bleed, yet nine months later he was back in the ring. His fans who were worried about him were relieved when Doyle won his next five fights leading up to the Robinson match. The Levine beating was more or less forgotten.

Fighting bravely but behind, Doyle was the victim of an awesome barrage by Sugar Ray in the eighth round. Doyle went down and never got up again. He died in the hospital the next day. Many boxing insiders at the time believed Sugar Ray only finished the job Artie Levine had started. That is where the entwinement existed between Sugar Ray and Artie Levine.

It's ironic, but time and again in boxing history, tragedies like Doyle vs. Robinson were repeated before and after this ill-fated bout going way back to the Jack Johnson era, when Jack's number-one contender took a tune-up fight with Arthur Pelkey, a ham-and-egger, before he was to engage Johnson in a title bout later that year. Luther McCarty was the great white hope. The first-round bell had barely faded away as the fighters clinched in ring center. Pelkey landed a halfhearted blow to McCarty's body. McCarty fell to the canvas and was counted out with boos and shouts of "fix" raining down on the ring. McCarty never got up again. He was carried out of the arena and laid down on the grass where he died. It was later learned that a few days before the fight, McCarty, a real cowboy, had been thrown from a horse and landed on his head. He dismissed the headache he had as nothing to jeopardize his upcoming fight.

Then there was the Primo Canera vs. Ernie Schaff fight, where light-hitting Primo dropped Schaff, a top contender, with a light left jab. Again amid fans' cry of "fake" and boos, Schaff was taken to the hospital, where he died. Most hard-core fans knew Ernie had taken a severe beating at the hands of kayo puncher Max Baer previously. The great French fighter Marcel Cerdan trounced rookie of the year LaVern Roach in the Garden. He dished out a bad beating to kayo the youngster. Roach came back to face Georgie Small, a fringe contender with a big punch. Roach was knocked out and died. Fans knew it was the Cerdan fight that started Roach on the way.

We could go on and on with these tragic results. Emile Griffith killed Benny Paret after Paret suffered a huge beating and kayo defeat at the hands of Gene Fullmer. Boxing has always been the "runt" of the litter when it comes to major sports. Baseball and football have national commissioners who run their sports with tough rules and regulations that are enforced to enhance the safety of their players. However in boxing, each state has a commissioner who has been appointed politically. The politicians use the job as a gift to a supporter who helped them in their election campaign. Many times a person is put into a job they know absolutely nothing about. Hence every state has different rules, sloppy safety methods, and complete idiots appointing inept people to the commission staff.

Who loses? The fighter and the fans. Boxing gets a bad name, and I blame it on the politics. The aforementioned fighters who died in the ring could have lived if knowledgeable people were in charge. If they had been given extensive and complete medical exams after their previous knockout loss, they could have had their license revoked until they were fit to box again. A national, knowledgeable commissioner would have the authority to see that an injured boxer would not be able to simply step back in the ring after a devastating knockdown loss in another state weeks earlier.

Things have not changed. Some states are piss-poor in their attempt to oversee boxing. There are a few good ones, but boxing needs a national czar.

Senator John McCain and Teddy Atlas have championed the cause for many years only to be lent a deaf ear from the bigwigs in Washington. It seems they dislike boxing and prefer to back Ping-Pong, golf, and tennis along with checkers as their favorite sports. God help the young athletes of America.

Getting back to Robinson vs. Doyle, Sugar was devastated as any fighter would be after an opponent succumbed to injuries received from his victory. He agreed to two fights for which his share of the purse was to go to Doyle's mother. One gets the feeling Sugar disliked working for nothing when he took out journeyman Sammy Secreet in one round and blasted out Flash Sebastian, a Philippine tomato can, in 62 seconds at MSG. The Flash was so fast no one saw his quick punches, neither Robinson nor the fans who attended the blowout. Flash was never seen or heard from again. Everyone was thankful Flash was able to get up after the ten count. They feared another Jimmy Doyle result.

Sugar was probably at his peak at this point of his career. His punching was sharp and crisp, very powerful.

He would defend his welterweight title five times before he was able to win the middleweight title from Jake LaMotta, which meant he had to relinquish the lower-weight championship. Sugar Ray didn't mind because he had to wear himself down to a frazzle to make the 147-pound weight limit.

Robinson's greatest fights were still ahead of him as a 160-pounder. Every fan of his is well schooled in his accomplishments after the 13th-round kayo of LaMotta, known as the "St. Valentine's Day Massacre."

The intent here was to focus on two of his fights that sort of fell through the cracks. It is my hope that this story brings the two fights into the proper perspective. Levine was his greatest fight; Doyle was his heartbreaker.

Robinson's lengthy career made him a wealthy man. He lived his life like a millionaire prince. On his European tour he went from country to country knocking out their champions, partying all the way. He had his famous "entourage" with him. These leeches drained Sugar, but Sugar only had to blame himself for allowing it to happen. He had his personal barber accompany him, along with his private physician and cooks, and also his masseur and trainers with sparring partners. Sugar paid all their bills plus a generous salary. The first two-month tour included six fights fought in five different countries, Sugar winning five with one no contest. That led up to the big finale fight in London against top-rated Randy Turpin. This fight was to complete his European tour before heading back to the states. Surprise! Randy upset the Great One for Sugar's second loss in 133 fights with a decision win. The entourage and the partying had taken their toll.

Two months later, Sugar won back his title, stopping Turpin in New York City's Polo Grounds. He went on with great fights against Bobo Olson, Rocky Graziano, Joey Maxim, Gene Fullmer and Carman Basilio. Two fights with Basilio were barnburner classics. Each won one. A rubber match was in demand by all. It never came off. Robinson wanted the lion's share of the purse. He finally met a man who was as stubborn as he was. Basilio wanted a 50/50 cut, as it should have been. Sugar refused, hoping Carman would settle for less, as so many did before him did. Basilio stuck to his guns, and only the fans and boxing lost that decision.

Sugar was 37 and should have retired after the second Basilio fight. It was the 1958 fight of the year, as was their first the year before. He would have left on a great note, having won his title back in a real classic. But no, Sugar fought on till he was 44 in a futile attempt to retain his exotic lifestyle.

He fought 50 more times after the second Basilio fight; 13 times he lost to fighters he wouldn't have accepted as sparring partners in his heyday. For instance he fought a loser named Young Joe Walcott in his last year, winning all three by decision. He could not knock out the perennial loser. The money he received for these fights was less than the tips he left in his big money days. His entourage deserted him as he hit hard times, fighting unknowns in small towns for peanuts. When he retired, all his money was gone. Sugar was broke.

In his career, Sugar fought everyone who could give him a fight. The better fighter, the more money he could make. Sugar knew that to become great you have to fight the very best. He barred no one.

Two fighters he missed, through no fault of his own, were Tony Zale and Marcel Cerdan. They would have given Sugar a battle, but when the dust settled it would be Sugar the winner.

Tony Zale burned himself out fighting Rocky Graziano in a trilogy that can't be forgotten. His last fight was a brutal kayo loss to Cerdan, who lost his life in an air crash. Then there was the third Basilio fight that never happened.

Your writer wished those fights had come off. They would have lifted boxing to new heights at the time. But how much can a fighter give? Sugar certainly gave his all, including in my opinion his greatest war with Artie Levine.

Frankie DePaula

Through the years there have been many tragic stories of boxers losing their lives by fatal accidents, suicides and, yes, hot lead from gang-related guns. We see it more in the sport of boxing than any other, but in recent years, NFL football is coming on strong with it and soon may be the leader.

People ask, *why*? Why is the ugly head of crime slowly but surely infesting our American athletes? We always wanted our heroes and heroines to be apple-pie American, the boy or girl next door–type, clean-cut role models for our children to admire.

Yet you can pick up the newspaper on any given day to find big-time athletes being arrested for drunk driving, drugs or common criminal behavior. Plus trash talk, which brings on diarrhea of the mouth. A lot of these guys are wealthy, some even millionaires from the money they made doing sports. Yet they can't get away from portraying themselves as thugs, which they may have been while growing up. Maybe it's true, you can't teach an old dog new tricks.

So it must have been with our subject in this story.

Frankie DePaula was a 175-pounder from Jersey City, New Jersey. Growing up in a tough neighborhood, Frankie belonged to gangs and spent a good part of his youth in reform schools. In short, he was a hell-raiser and a great street fighter. He could punch like a demon. Few people messed with Frankie; he was a true badass.

His street brawl success got Frankie to thinking he could make some money by flattening people. He decided to fight professionally. After a brief but winning amateur record, he turned pro at the age of 22, a little late, but if he could showcase his knockout punch, he knew it would move him fast through the ranks.

I first saw Frankie in his second pro fight at the Gladiators' Arena,

Totowa, New Jersey. His opponent, Mike Pacheco, who also was fighting his second pro bout, was one hell of a tough cookie. He and Frankie engaged in an all-out, slam-bang war. No soft touches for Frankie, he had to go all out to earn the *draw* of four rounds. The fight called for a rematch, which was held two weeks later, again a huge barn burner. Frankie edged out Pacheco for the four-round decision.

Right then and there I picked Frankie DePaula as a future star. He reminded me of another Rocky Graziano coming up. I also thought Pacheco could make waves in the future. Funny thing is, I never heard of Mike Pacheco again. It's possible he decided there were easier ways of making a living than getting bombed with DePaula right hands. Keeping tabs on Frankie, I noticed he was scoring kayo wins and was moving fast. In only his seventh pro fight, he was already fighting eight-rounders. He fought to a draw in this one with Haywood Johnson. In his 11th fight he held the highly touted boxer-puncher Don McAteer to a draw at Teaneck, New Jersey. I was at ringside for their fight and also for the return bout two months later. Both fights were classics which were described earlier in this book.

The belief here is that Frankie and his handlers knew, since he got the decision over McAteer in the return, that Frankie could mingle with the division's very best. I also believed DePaula was now at the turning point of his career.

He would drop a decision now and again to slick boxers, much like Rocky Graziano did early on in his career. Rocky hated boxers who would run, and so did Frankie.

After the McAteer fights, Frankie started fighting with much more belief in himself. His team started taking more fights for Frankie out of state. DePaula lost a few decisions but then put together five straight knockout wins, the last three at Madison Square Garden, New York. The wins were so impressive Frankie earned a fight with Dick Tiger, former middleweight and light heavyweight champion of the world. Tiger was a solid rough, tough fighter who was said to never have been floored in over 70-odd fights. In a wild and wooly brawl Frankie floored the Tiger two times in the second round. Tiger returned in the third round to drop DePaula two times, getting even with the young slugger. The fight went on to the tenth and final round with Tiger earning the decision. The fight was named the 1968 fight of the year by *Ring* magazine.

DePaula's last four fights packed the Garden. His terrific punching style brought in the fans to the box office. Bob Foster, the reigning light heavyweight champion, was in need of a challenger he could make money with. Foster was one of the greatest light heavy kings that ever lived. He was a deadly puncher.

He had cleaned out his division of worthy challengers. Although DePaula was the loser against Tiger, he was offered a title shot at Foster at the Garden.

The fight was made for January 1969, just three months after the great war of Tiger-DePaula. That fight was fresh in the minds of fans, who believed the huge underdog DePaula had a punchers' chance at upsetting the apple cart. With these two bombers, there was no way the fight could possibly go the full 15 rounds.

The first-round bell sounded and all hell broke loose. DePaula floored the great Bob Foster, who got up in a furious rage, less hurt than embarrassed. He dropped Frankie three times for the idiotic three-knockdown rule to kick in. I believe one knockdown was the result of a push. Through the years I've seen many fights ruined with that silly rule. In time, most states did away with it.

The fight only lasted a little over two minutes, but Frankie's punching power was on the way to making him a superstar. His two losing fights to Tiger and Foster only made him more popular. The future looked good for Frankie. He continued with two more kayo wins, and then the crap hit the fan.

Evidently Frankie was still mixed up with the gangs. He was arrested for being part of a theft ring. He posted bail and was free pending trial.

His fellow gang members figured with Frankie being so popular and in reach of lucrative paydays (he had a fight scheduled with Don Fullmer at Madison Square Garden), he just might make a deal with the law to turn state's evidence. With this in mind, Frankie DePaula was gunned down on a city street by his mob friends. The hit man did not accomplish his goal. Frankie was still alive but in critical condition, hanging on to life by a thread. He lived in this condition for almost a year before death took him on September 14, 1970. Frankie was just 31 years old. What a complete waste.

DePaula had two ways to go. Two roads, one to the right which would certainly lead to riches and an enjoyable life. He chose the left with his old habits and shit-bird friends.

It was sad to see it happen. Frankie was an exciting fighter to watch, and his punch was getting stronger as he met stiffer competition. He was coming along just like Rocky Graziano did. Rocky had a turning-point fight with Billy Arnold, a huge favorite over the Rock in their Garden fight. Rocky, after an early beating, came back like gangbusters and flattened Arnold. He never looked back and went on to win the title.

DePaula's turning point was the Don McAteer fights, after which it looked like he was going the way of Rocky.

The fact is Rocky took the right road that led to the title and TV with his many commercials, which made him a millionaire. Their careers were very similar to a point. Only, Frankie could not shake off his past as Rocky did.

I recall one night at Totowa, attending the fights, we fight buffs gathered in the back of the arena to talk fights before the show. In the crowd I spotted DePaula; it was the first time I seen him up close. I didn't realize, but I must have been staring at him. Our eyes made contact. His look and body language suggested, "What the hell are you looking at?" I quickly turned away and went to my seat. I knew this man's reputation, and I knew he'd fight at the drop of a hat. I wanted nothing to do with him as far as fisticuffs went. I also knew he still maintained that bully attitude—this at a time when his boxing career was blossoming with his string of Garden kayos.

That might have been the tip-off of things to come. His success had not changed his old ways as it should have.

God Bless you, Frankie; you provided us with many thrills.

More Thumbnail Sketches

It would be cruel of your writer to ignore the following fighters who gave their sweat and blood while clawing and scrambling their way to main-event status. Some made it; most didn't. However, they left their mark on Jersey boxing. The fight fans were treated to great slam-bang action on the undercards of the main events. Without these warriors, boxing would die. They became fan favorites and kept the turnstiles humming and the fans' butts in the seats. Which made promoters excel by bringing in the very best to headline their cards. Thus the fans made out big time.

Randy Neumann

New Jersey boxing can always take pride in the fact that Randy Neumann is one of our own.

Born in Cliffside Park, New Jersey, Randy was, and is, a credit to the sport. This intelligent, well-spoken, well-read man could have done well in any sport. He had the athletic ability. Yet he decided on boxing, considered by many as a violent, barbaric sport that highly educated people avoided.

I guess Randy liked the one-on-one and the true excitement physical combat brings. Plus the feeling only a winner can feel after a solid win. Self-confidence and satisfaction with oneself. Quite a reward gained.

His first pro bout was a one-round knockout victory scored at Madison Square Garden. He fought there often. I attended his fight there against Junior Wilkeson, Randy taking the decision. His biggest win at the Garden was over Jimmy Young, a ten-round win. The same Young was the fighter who gave Muhammad Ali fits and defeated George Foreman and sent him into retirement.

Other big wins he scored were over Chuck Wepner, Pedro Agosto and Boone Kirkman. He left boxing in 1977 after a credible pro career. He became a notable referee and writer in much demand to this day.

Big Bill Gilliam

This East Orange, New Jersey, heavyweight was the most puzzling case I have ever encountered. I called him the "heavy who no one knew." This 6'2", 215-pound contender was considered huge at the time. Thus the name "Big Bill." With today's heavies, he would be considered average size.

He was a coworker of mine in a Linden, New Jersey, warehouse. He was very quiet, this good man of a few words. Bill was overwhelmed when I first introduced myself to him and presented him with photos and clips of some of his fights. He couldn't believe someone remembered him enough to collect memorabilia of him. Few of the other employees even knew he was a fighter. Bill never bragged about himself. Needless to say, we became fast friends, and Bill confided in me. He walked me through the heavyweight division of his time when he fought them all—stories of his fights and little known facts about his opponents.

Big Bill fought and beat Nino Valdes, Hein Ten Hoff, Bob Baker, Omelio Agra Monte, Lenard Morrow (who was a one-round kayo winner over Archie Moore), Willie Bean and Red Applegate. Ten Hoff was the German champion who lost a tight decision to Jersey Joe Walcott. Bill kayoed the German. He fought Able Cestac, the highly touted Argentine champ, to a draw at Laurel Garden. Bill lost decisions to champs Ezzard Charles and Harold Johnson. I often asked him who was the hardest puncher he ever faced. His answer, "they all hit hard."

He was mostly ignored by the boxing writers of the day as if he didn't exist. He went unnoticed, with hardly any recognition his entire career. For this I detected a bit of bitterness in the hardworking gentle giant.

Mike DeCosmo, the Southpaw

Mike DeCosmo, the Elizabeth, New Jersey, welterweight hailing from the Peterstown section of the city, was a hard-hitting crowd favorite. He fought in the late '40s and early '50s, a stable mate of Gus Lesnivich, the world's light heavyweight champion, and managed by the crafty Joe Vella.

Old-timers of that period would recall Mike, as the fine fighter he was, battling the best at a time when there was an overabundance of fistic talent to compete against.

His standout wins over Tony Riccio, Norman Rubio and two knock-outs over the undefeated Tommy Parks, which ended that great prospect's career, were very notable. Holding Earnie "the Rock" Durando to a draw was the highlight of his career, given the fact he gave the Rock, a murderous puncher, a seven-pound weight advantage. They packed the arena. Many fans were turned away. Both visited the canvas in the bloody eight-round draw. Durando won the rematch by kayo in another bloodbath to an overflowing crowd at Jersey City.

Mike left the sport at the top of his game. What happened was Mike fell in love and got married. His young bride insisted he give up boxing and go into business, which Mike did. He was a success at that too.

Stefen Redl

A Hungarian who came to the United States in the 1950s and settled in New Jersey. Redl started his pro career like a cyclone, winning his first 17 fights, 13 by kayo.

Two of those kayo victories over Al Milone, an all-action fighter like Steve, were all-out wars. They made Redl a New Jersey favorite; the fans adored his aggressive style.

Redl became a favorite at St. Nicholas Arena in New York, scoring many good wins there. He fought the best and beat a lot of them. He could not reach that very top level; he lost the "big ones," although he gave his best shots to succeed. He left boxing in the early 1960s with an admirable record and for his fans the memories of his action-packed fights.

I met Stefen Redl in 2006 at a boxing dinner. He appeared bright-eyed and bushy tailed. We talked boxing, and he was very gracious to pose for pictures with me.

Willis "Red" Applegate

A Montclair, New Jersey, heavyweight who before boxing starred in the All-Negro Pro Baseball League for Newark. He turned to boxing in 1946. His main claim to fame was he became one of five men to take Rocky Marciano to scorecards, in a 1951 fight at Providence, Rhode Island, losing a unanimous ten-round decision. Earlier he had also taken Philly's "Black Jack" Billy Fox to his first decision in 45 fights and scored the upset win in my hometown of Elizabeth, New Jersey. He fought a number of times in Laurel Garden main events. He lost to Archie McBride for the vacant New Jersey heavyweight title. Other big names he fought were Gus Dorazio, Billy Gilliam, Leo Matriciani, Lee Oma and Jimmy Bivins.

After his retirement we met up at the warehouse where I worked. Red came in as a helper to a trucker many times. I knew him immediately; he was an albino with red hair and a creamy white complexion. He was obsessed with Rocky Marciano, telling my coworkers tall tales of him dropping Rocky in gym workouts and being robbed of the decision in their fight.

Sometime later we learned he was found dead alongside the railroad tracks. It was unclear if it was murder, suicide or an accident.

Roger Murial

Roger was an awkwardly clever middleweight from Elizabeth, New Jersey. Sadly, he never became the star his talents and potential seemingly destined him to be. He didn't have the right connections a fighter should have to "move" him along. It was a fact that Roger was avoided by most fighters in his day simply because of his "spoiler" style.

Fights were hard to come by for Roger, and he jumped at any offer he received. One such offer came in the form of Ernie "the Rock" Durando, Bayonne kayo artist.

Roger outpointed the "Rock" over eight rounds in a huge upset. A few days later Roger walked into the gym as Pete Nozza was putting Phil Saxton through his paces. In feigning unbearable horror, Roger gave out a scream and ran back out the door. When questioned of his antics, Roger claimed Pete Nozza was a dead ringer for Ernie Durando, the handsome puncher he had upset. Roger was still hurting from the Rock's bombs and didn't want to see or hear from him again. A compliment to Ernie's punching power.

Mr. Boxing of New Jersey—Paul Venti

With the news of the sudden passing of Paul Venti, my heart became heavy with sadness. What could I do or say? A reflex took me to pen and paper. My thoughts of this fine gentleman had to be recorded for my boxing archives. After all, he was Mr. Boxing of New Jersey, a man whom I met and conversed with only a few times. Amazingly, he and I bonded almost immediately. My regret is the friendship was so short lived. I honestly wished I had met him years before.

Here was a man who loved the sport of boxing as much as I do. Our very first conversation led me to believe he was bitten by the so-called boxing bug early in life. Those of us so bitten always retain the unexplained, extreme and intense fondness and devotion to our sport for our entire lives. We eat, drink, sleep, talk and live boxing. We defend it with a passion. I doubt any other sport has that effect on a fan.

Watching Paul at boxing dinners, I admired his zest and zeal while performing his tasks at those functions. I saw a man who was completely happy and fulfilled helping his beloved sport.

When talking with Paul, he had me amazed with all the fighters he knew personally. My respect for him was unlimited. For years I'd seen him referee and judge fights, but I didn't know him at that time. I consider myself cheated for missing out.

We met at a Ring 25 dinner in 2002. From that time on, Paul became one of a special group of once-bitten boxing buffs whom I recall each time the "sweet science" is on display.

Paul and this elite group are remembered each time I hear the rat-a-tat-tat of a speed bag. The thud of a powerful punch into a heavy-bag, the pounding of the pads, and the scuffle of boxing shoes on a gym floor as boxers shadowboxed. The roar of the crowd, the ringside bell. All sounds of the sport he loved. Rest in peace, Paul. To your family I extend my sincerest condolences.

Boxing Trivia

1. Who was the only fighter to hold a knockout win over the great Jack Dempsey?

2. Name the two fighters who became Academy Award winners.

3. What heavyweight contender died in the electric chair?

4. What heavyweight title challenger lost seventeen times by knockout before challenging for the championship?

5. Who was the fighter who fought Jack Dempsey four times and only lost once?

6. Sandy Sadler was kayoed only once in 163 fights. In his second pro fight he was knocked out by an opponent who went on to challenge Willie Pep in a title bout. Who was he?

7. Who was the first man to defeat Sugar Ray Robinson?

8. Who kayoed Muhammad Ali in the amateurs?

9. In the movie *The Joe Louis Story*, who portrayed Joe?

10. What fighter went the ten-round distance *twice* with Rocky Marciano?

11. What fighter challenged for the title with a perfect 43–0 record, all by knockout?

12. Kid Gavilan in his entire career of over a hundred fights was never knocked out. He was floored only twice. Who were the two fighters that dropped the Kid?

13. What was Sugar Ray Robinson's real name?

14. Who was the only fighter to have fought both Jack Dempsey and Joe Louis? He was knocked out by both.

15. In Joe Louis's twenty-five title defenses, five contenders fought Joe twice. Name them.

16. What fighter beat Kid Gavilan on the Kid's way up and again while he was on top. Kid could not beat this very ordinary fighter, dropping two ten-round decisions to him.

17. Who was the first man to defeat Willie Pep, halting Willie's streak at 62?

18. What fighter holds the record of consecutive knockout wins in Madison Square Garden main events?

19. Three former middleweight champs committed suicide. Name them.

20. Sugar Ray Robinson defended his world welterweight title by knocking out this challenger, who died of injuries received in the fight. Name him.

21. There were three fighting Fullmer Brothers. Gene, Don and one other. Name the third.

22. What fighter kayoed Sonny Liston and never fought again?

23. Early in his career this fighter was called "The One-Man Gang from the Bronx," and later the "Raging Bull." Who is he?

24. Name the heavyweight champs who killed men in the ring.

25. Who was Sonny Liston's last opponent?

26. Who had the most fights of all heavyweight champions?

27. What was Joe Louis's real name?

28. Joe Louis fought a New Jersey heavyweight in a ten-round no-decision fight at Newark Armory. Name him.

29. What light heavyweight champion on his way up was kayoed by Jersey Joe Walcott who also kayoed his father? Both father and son went in three rounds.

30. English heavyweight champion Joe Bugner lost decisions to a father-and-son team. Who were they?

31. Who was the first heavyweight champion to regain the title?

32. When Emile Griffith was named fighter of the year, he was promptly flattened in the first round of his next fight. Who kayoed him?

33. Marvin Hagler used the same trainer/managers his entire career. Who were they?

34. What great Filipino fighter died from an abscessed tooth?

35. Bob Hope fought under what name?

36. What heavyweight contender was billed out of Cut and Shoot, Texas?

37. What was Tony Zale's real name?

38. What welterweight champion, before winning that title, lost to Tippy Larkin five times?

39. Who was Marcel Cerdan's opponent in his American debut?

40. Who was the only fighter to floor Jake LaMotta?

41. What American fight had the highest attendance?

42. What middleweight champ died in a plane crash?

43. Who fought Sugar Ray Robinson in Robinson's last fight?

44. Which fight was boxing's first million-dollar gate?

45. Rocky Marciano ended a very promising fighter's career with a brain injury. Name that fighter.

46. What great trainer actually molded Marciano into the deadly fighting machine he was?

47. Name the fighter who died of injuries at the hands of Primo Carnera.

48. Who was the referee who had a heatstroke during the Robinson vs. Maxim fight and had to be replaced?

49. Name the American Olympic heavyweight champion who turned pro and was killed in the ring.

50. Joe Louis defended his title a record twenty-five times. Only two of his challengers were black. Name them.

Boxing Trivia Answers

1. Fireman Jim Flynn
2. Victor McLaglen and Jack Palance
3. Henry "Snow" Flakes
4. Lee Oma, vs. champ Ezzard Charles
5. Willie Meeham
6. Jock Leslie, Flint, Michigan
7. Jake LaMotta
8. Kent Green
9. Coley Wallace
10. Tiger Ted Lowry
11. Black Jack Billy Fox
12. Ike Williams and Carmen Basilio
13. Walker Smith
14. Jack Sharkey
15. Arturo Godoy, Abe Simon, Buddy Baer, Billy Conn, and Jersey Joe Walcott
16. Doug Ratford
17. Sammy Angott
18. Rocky Graziano
19. Kid McCoy, Billy Papke, and Randy Turpin
20. Jimmy Doyle
21. Jay Fullmer

22. Leotis Martin

23. Jake LaMotta

24. Max Baer, Primo Carnera, Jess Willard, Ezzard Charles, and Bob Fitzsimmons

25. Chuck Wepner

26. Ezzard Charles

27. Joseph Louis Barrow

28. Bayonne's Joe Cheshul

29. Harold Johnson

30. Joe and Marvis Frazier

31. Floyd Patterson

32. Rubin "Hurricane" Carter

33. The Petronelli brothers, Goodie and Pat

34. Poncho Villa

35. Packy East

36. Roy Harris

37. Anthony Florian Zaleski

38. Freddie "Red" Cochrane

39. George Abrams

40. Danny Nardico

41. Tony Zale–Billy Pryor. It was free.

42. Marcel Cerdan

43. Joey Archer

44. Jack Dempsey vs. Georges Carpentier

45. Carmine Vingo

46. Charley Goldman

47. Ernie Schaaf

48. Ruby Goldstein

49. Ed Sanders

50. John Henry Lewis and Jersey Joe Walcott

Index

193